ASOKA THE GREAT

IMMORTALS OF HISTORY

ASOKA THE GREAT
India's Royal Missionary

by

Emil Lengyel

Franklin Watts, Inc.
575 Lexington Avenue
New York, N.Y. 10022

Other *Immortals* by the author:

JAWAHARLAL NEHRU
LAJOS KOSSUTH
MAHATMA GANDHI

To Dr. Shantiswarup Gupta,
scholar and diplomat,
learned admirer of Asoka

Cover photograph courtesy
Press Information Bureau,
Government of India

CONTENTS

INTRODUCTION

HISTORY knows him as Asoka the Great, maharaja, great ruler of the kingdom of Magadha in India. His domains also included distant regions beyond the confines of the Indian peninsula. Sometimes he was called emperor and sometimes king. In his younger days he was also called *Candasoka*—"Evil Asoka." That was before he had a change of heart and entered history as *Dharmasoka*—"Good Asoka." History has recorded few changes of this kind in the conduct of a king. He ruled twenty-two centuries ago for a period of some forty years. The record is somewhat blurred—it was such a long time ago. Yet, he has never been forgotten, not only in India, but in other parts of the world as well.

Asoka's name has not been forgotten because, even though he lived so many centuries ago, he was a "modern" man. In an age when the common man counted for little, Asoka upheld the dignity of man, no matter what his birth. That is why he has been hailed as a unique ruler. England's famous writer H. G. Wells wrote about him: "The name of Asoka shines and shines alone, a star. From the Volga to Japan his name is still honored.

. . . More living men cherish his memory today than ever heard the names of Constantine or Charlemagne."

A similar view was expressed by the noted archeologist Peter I. von Koeppen: "If a man's fame can be measured by the number of hearts that revere his memory, by the number of lips that have mentioned and still mention him with honor, Asoka is more famous than Charlemagne or Caesar."

And this tribute from a leading missionary, James M. MacPhail: "In the history of ancient India the figure of Asoka stands out like some great Himalayan peak, clear against the sky, resplendent in the sun, while the lower and nearer ranges are hidden by the clouds."

History likes to honor great warriors—Alexander the Great, Julius Caesar, Napoleon—by remembering their victories. This is not so with Asoka. Although he was indeed a warrior at the outset, and a very good one at that, the immortality he gained was not because of the blood he had caused to be shed on the battlefield. He gained fame because, in an age of war, he sought to turn the peoples' minds to peace. He is remembered, too, because he promoted a creed that tried to convince the people of the world to live in amity.

Asoka embraced that creed—a minor sect called Buddhism—and turned it into a major religion of the world, as it is today. It was to be a religion of peace and brotherly love. With Asoka's aid, Buddhism spread from the Indian peninsula into China, Japan, and Southeast Asia, across Asia's soaring mountains and vast seas. To Buddhism, Asoka was what Saint Paul and Emperor

Constantine were to Christianity centuries later—an immortal missionary. The records of Asoka's achievements were carved into pillars and rocks, many of them preserved to this very day. They contain the details of the stunning "Asoka story." They demonstrate his greatest achievement—a king's concern for his fellowmen.

ASOKA THE GREAT

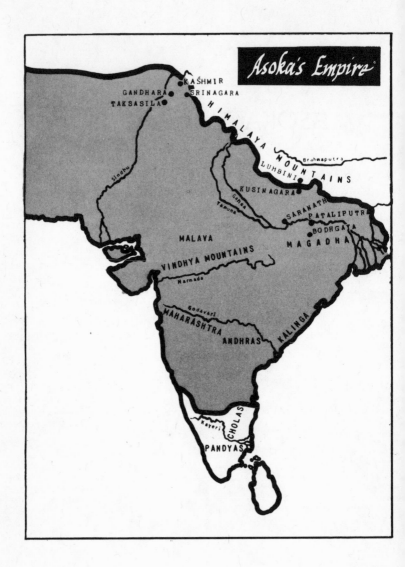

Asoka's Empire

1

✒ IT ALL BEGAN WITH ALEXANDER

THERE might never have been a historic age of Asoka the Great without Alexander the Great. Yet, the homes of these men were worlds apart. Asoka's home was in India, in the valley of the river Ganges, while Alexander came from Macedonia, the northern highlands of Greece. Also, Alexander lived a century before Asoka. Yet, it was because of the lasting influence of the Macedonian that the foundations of Asoka's historic role could be laid. To understand Asoka, we must first take a look at Alexander and his contact with India.

As a boy of sixteen, Alexander, the son of Philip II of Macedon, probably had no idea about the location of India. But already at that age he displayed such qualities of leadership that his royal father appointed him a regent of his realm. Four years later, in 336 B.C., Philip was dead by an assassin's hand, and Alexander began the fantastic career which was to take him to India and link his story with Asoka's. Alexander was now called king of Macedon, captain general of the Hellenes (Greeks), and head of the Panhellenic League. He was not yet known as ruler of the world, but he was headed in that direction at the age of twenty-two. There was no holding him back; he felt the strength to rule the world.

Outside of Greece, Egypt and Mesopotamia were then considered the pivotal portions of the world. Irresistibly, the young warlord swept into Egypt, the Land of the Nile, and made such an impression upon its people that he was worshiped there as a god. From the Nile, he stormed into Mesopotamia, Land of the Two Rivers—Tigris and Euphrates—considered the Hinge of the World. The possession of these regions enabled the youthful conqueror to make his bid for the highest prize.

In his attempt to become the master of the world, Alexander could be challenged only by Persia, the great power of the East. Persia's King Darius was a warrior of fabulous fame, and so redoubtable were members of his bodyguard that the people called them immortals. But, in the face of the young hero from Macedon, they turned out to be men of clay.

A born leader of men, Alexander had two paramount qualities of leadership: he inspired the confidence of his followers; and he sized up opportunities with lightninglike speed. Aided by these qualities, he promptly found the enemy's weakest spot and managed to demoralize his forces. What was the sense of resisting this godlike creature? The crucial battle against the Persians was fought on the banks of the Tigris, and again the godlike hero won. Darius fled, and vanished into the mountains. Having been defeated in the crucial fight, the Persian lost face, and it was his own "immortals" who took his life.

Alexander resumed his victorious march, and while doing so he not only destroyed but also created. As he crushed the hostile forces, he also perpetuated his own memory by founding countless cities that were to carry his name. Thus it was that he founded, among many other towns, Alexandria, Egypt's great seaport near the estuary of the Nile, and also Alexandretta, a port in modern Turkey. Alexander was accompanied not only by town planners but also by scholars. Meanwhile, the Macedonian soldiers became bloated with the spoils of war.

Where was the "end" of the world that Alexander was to conquer? Having subdued Persia, the army of the young warlord crossed the scorched land of the Afghans. From there it descended into the Punjab—Land of Five Rivers—watered by the river Indus. This was India. Was this the end of the world?

Many of Alexander's soldiers thought so. They shared a broadly held superstition that the border of the world was the fathomless sea on one side and an unscalable mountain range on the other. It was not just any kind of mountain. The range contained great peaks from which wrathful demons, using thunder and lightning, could destroy people who sought to penetrate their secrets. As for the sea, it was different, too. Unlike the blue waters of the Mediterranean, with which the soldiers were familiar, the waves of this sea were said to be the darkest black, exhaling deadly fumes.

Alexander, surrounded by his scholars, did not share these superstitions. The land toward the rising sun, the heartland of India—his scholars told him—contained a vast depository of some of the world's most precious gems. The maharajas, great rulers, with their bejeweled garments, were some of the richest people in the world.

In an attempt to push all the way to the end of the world, the forces of Alexander penetrated into the Punjab, ruled by Paurava raja, whom the Greeks called Porus. His domains clustered around the Jhelum River, a major tributary of the Indus. Alexander felt that if he could defeat Porus, a doughty warrior, the gates of the rest of India would be open. The Macedonian warlord had moved easily from victory to victory, and now, in 326 B.C., he faced the greatest challenge of his career.

The forces of Porus were defending their own homeland. If they survived a defeat, they knew that they might be dragged thousands of miles away from home, to end their lives in slavery. They had not been fatigued, as the challengers had been, by forced marches across uncharted lands, constantly moving away from home year after year. Porus was reported to have some thirty thousand fresh and well-trained troops, supported by additional thousands of men and three hundred war chariots capable of striking like a bolt from the sky. Besides, Porus had hundreds of battle-trained elephants that could trample an entire army to death, a formidable force to strike terror into even the stoutest hearts. The massive force of elephants might also serve as a solid wall of defense.

It was Alexander's strategy never to give the foe a chance to gain momentum by seizing the initiative. The Macedonian was always the one to strike first. On this crucial day, what part of the enemy's force was he to try to demolish? He decided to hit the foe at his strongest point—the solid wall of elephants. His own veterans wondered whether he knew what he was doing. He did.

Taken by surprise, the elephants broke ranks and started to stampede, trampling many of Porus' stalwarts underfoot. Against hopeless odds, the Indian ruler kept up the fight, seeking death on the battlefield rather than to wear the yoke of the slave. Within hours he lost twenty thousand foot soldiers, three thousand horsemen, and his chariots. His two sons also lost their lives. He was badly wounded but still conscious enough to hope for a mercifully quick death.

But Porus did not die. Instead, he was captured, his life at the mercy of the Macedonian warlord. In this instance, too, Alexander showed that he deserved to be hailed as great. Respecting the valor of his foe, he summoned medical help to save Porus' life. The fear of the

defeated man was not justified. Instead of being enslaved, he was asked to become an adviser to the noble
victor.

This time the best part of India, the fertile valley of
the Ganges, the fabulous land of unfathomable wealth,
lay open to the Greeks. Farther east they faced the army
of the Indian kingdom of Magadha, ruled by the Nanda
dynasty, and supported by a force of 200,000 foot soldiers, 20,000 cavalry, 3,000 chariots, and 4,000 elephants,
veterans of many successful battles. These forces were
far more numerous than those of Alexander's. But then
he was used to winning over superior forces. What foe
could resist him?

One foe did resist him—his own soldiers. They had
endured unbearable hardships, having covered thousands
of miles across the world's tallest mountains, down the
baking deserts of sandy plains, tormented by all the elements. Many of the veterans were now dead, while
others were the victims of strange ailments in a strange
world. Many feared the demons dwelling in the mountain ranges at the end of the world. They also feared
the dark waves of the endless seas. Too long had they
been carrying the spoils, and now the time had come to
return home. The homeward journey would take years.

Undefeated by the mighty potentates of the world,
Alexander was defeated by his own men. They refused to
follow him into the land of untold dangers and untold
wealth. He had to turn back and strike out for home
in great haste, down the rivers of the Punjab, across
the Persian deserts and mountain peaks. It took the

army two years to reach Mesopotamia, and in Babylon the tired warriors stopped to rest. It was there that the most fabulous career of the age saw its dramatic end. Alexander died in June, 323 B.C., after having conquered all the world considered worthy of being won. He was dead at the age of thirty-three.

But in a sense he did not die. Certainly he did not die to the people who decided that he was too much of a god to have a human end. So great was the respect even of the defeated Persians for him that they turned him into their own god. In a strange reversion of beliefs, people venerated him as the divine son of Darius, who had lost that crucial battle.

Although Alexander lived more than three centuries before Christ, he came to be venerated as a saint by Christian monks. In the same way, he came to be venerated by the Muslims, and was considered an aid of Muhammad, founder of their religion, who lived centuries after Alexander's death. Veneration was also accorded to him by the offspring of other people whose ancestors he had slaughtered. The local variety of the name of Alexander—Iskander—became a popular name for boys. An often-heard blessing voiced the hope: "May the child grow up to be as heroic as his namesake."

The death of Alexander the Great did not sever the relations of the Greek and Indian worlds. After his victory over Porus, many of the local great rulers rallied to his cause. Before leaving India, he set up vice-regencies there. These were successful for a time in keeping the great rulers from fighting one another, so that the bloodshed, normal in that age in those regions, was averted. At that point the history of Alexander the Great became entwined with that of Asoka the Great. The Macedonian had shown that it was possible to create conditions of peace in India. The way to do that was to unite the feuding kingdoms. And the lesson was learned by Asoka years later, even though after Alexander the component parts of the north Indian realm reverted to their previous habits. Alexander's vice-regencies were removed, and the colonies he established in India failed to take roots. This failure justified the pessimistic view of Vincent A. Smith, the British historian: "The campaign [of Alexander], although carefully designed to secure a permanent conquest, was in actual fact no more than a brilliantly successful raid on a gigantic scale which left upon India no mark save the horrid scars of bloody war."

While that was true, it was no less true that Alexander had demonstrated the feasibility of uniting the many tribes of northern India. Had the great warlord lived, he might have been able to keep the area together. Alexander's Indian campaign showed the way to future indigenous leaders. If they could bring about such a union, then India's resistance to outside pressure would be greatly strengthened.

The lesson taught by Alexander the Great was remembered in the kingdom of Magadha, which had been spared the test of facing the fabulous Macedonian. A century later the king of Magadha had his chance to follow in the footsteps of Alexander. History was to know this ruler as Asoka the Great.

2

✂ A NEW DYNASTY TO
THE FORE

KING Dhana Nanda had committed an inexcusable error. He had slighted a prominent Brahman, a member of the priestly caste of the Hindu religion. This particular Brahman also had the reputation of being a philosopher. The king should have known that nothing was more dangerous than a philosopher's wrath.

The king ruled over much of the Ganges Valley. In the fourth century before the Christian era, the peninsula of India contained "good" and "bad" regions. Good applied to the areas in which the soil was fertile. The best part of India was situated in the valley of the Ganges (Indians call it "Ganga") in the north. The kingdom of

Magadha was situated in the northeastern part of the river valley, roughly in the area of the modern state of Bihar. Because the water of the river sustained life for millions, it was considered sacred, and so it is regarded to this very day. The capital of the kingdom was Patali-putra—today's city of Patna.

It must have been a stately place, stretching along the riverfront for over ten miles. The city was protected by a deep moat, strengthened by a stout palisade of the hardest timber, with 570 towers manned by crack arch-ers. The capital is reported to have had no fewer than 64 gates linking it to its hinterland. Defense was the keynote of the city's life, and for good reasons. Patali-putra was in the very midst of a fruitful land, well tended by an industrious peasantry. Other dwellers of the plains clung to their wandering life. Cattle formed the chief wealth of these people, and one of their words for war literally meant "desire for cows."

Besides the farmers and ranchers, Magadha also had inhabitants engaged in a variety of occupations: black-smiths, coppersmiths, goldsmiths, barbers, carpenters, and other artisans. The king appears to have been the paramount chief. Each father of the family was the priest of his own household, but women also enjoyed a high position.

Magadha was the most important of the four mon-archies in the region because of the Ganges River, the quality of the soil, and the situation of the capital. The king, therefore, had a chance to enjoy a prosperous life. But Dhana Nanda made the great mistake, as we have seen, of affronting a revengeful philosopher. The name of the philosopher was Kautalya, and his revenge changed the fate of the kingdom.

It was the custom of the king to call crown council meetings, at which he would listen to the advice of his sages, including Kautalya, the Brahman. At the end of the meetings the king usually distributed gifts among them. This time he not only withheld the usual gift from Kautalya, but told the Brahman that his advice made no sense. Kautalya was an oversensitive man, and he stormed out of the council chamber, swearing revenge. And it followed in a devious way.

One day, nursing his grudge, Kautalya was roaming in a clump of woods when he came across a young boy playing kings-at-court. Greatly interested, the Brahman met the family of the boy, too, and from them he learned that they were of royal blood. They had been ousted from their chieftain position by the Nandas. This was welcome news to the philosopher. He drew the conclusion that Dhana Nanda, the ruler who had slighted him, was a mere impostor, and that the boy was the rightful heir to the throne. The name of the youth was Chandragupta Maurya, who, with the help of the philosopher, was to play a vital role in the history of India.

Kautalya set out to groom the boy to fulfill the role for which he had been destined by his origin. He acquainted him with the history of his family, inculcating the idea in his mind that the throne of Magadha was his birthright. This happened about the time that Alexander the Great was making his mark on India, planting garrisons, concluding alliances, and establishing military settlements. Chandragupta, an energetic youth, is said to have met the great Macedonian, who encouraged him to oust the usurper and to unite the states of the Ganges Valley.

Ambitious and old beyond his years, Chandragupta learned much from Alexander. He learned to accept life's challenges and responsibility, to secure the loyalty of his aides, and, above all, to trust only himself. He also learned the advantages of one united kingdom instead of many. The more states in India the greater was the friction among them, entailing wars, with the inevitable loss of money and lives.

King Dhana Nanda unintentionally helped the boy by committing even more stupidities. He kept affronting influential people, thus creating an army of foes. He let incompetents run the country, while he himself led an easy life, with little work and much pleasure. He increased the taxes constantly to pay for his life of ease. Although he had been an effective ruler, now he was losing his grip, and his subjects were becoming increasingly discontented.

Young Chandragupta knew that the time to strike was when the subjects of the king were ready for a change. He organized a force of ambitious young men, acquainted them with his claim to the throne, and promised them rich rewards. Finally, the auspicious moment arrived and the plotters attacked the royal stronghold. They were successful in gaining control of numerous strategic points in the royal capital, but they failed elsewhere and were routed while trying to rally their forces for the final onslaught. Chandragupta himself barely escaped with his life.

At this point, he might have decided to abandon his ambitious design. But he had learned from the example of Alexander that the price of success was persistence. Biding his time for a favorable moment, he struck again, and this time he and his warriors broke the resistance of the royal archers. Quickly they penetrated into the king's chambers and slayed him. The work of revenge was accomplished when, in 321 B.C., the Nanda dynasty was overthrown and Chandragupta Maurya ascended the Magadha throne.

Chandragupta had also learned a lesson from Alexander the Great which he promptly began to apply against the great Macedonian's successor. He was Seleucus I, ruler of the regions adjacent to north India. It was the aim of Seleucus to penetrate farther east into India, seeking to reach the "end of the world." This doughty ruler who called himself Nicator—the Victor—made an attempt to subdue Chandragupta. But he was not the conqueror he had imagined himself to be, and he lost.

Chandragupta had the good sense not to force his luck too far, and he concluded an agreement with the conquered "victor." He received the Punjab in northwestern India, and also the Kabul Valley, a part of what is Afghanistan today. He also received Beluchistan, the land in between. In exchange, he gave Seleucus five hundred elephants. To top off this one-sided arrangement,

Chandragupta was given the daughter of Seleucus as his wife.

The two rulers exchanged ambassadors, and that turned out to be a boon for posterity. The Greek ambassador was Megasthenes, a competent historian who recorded his impressions of the Chandragupta court. Until then, the West had known little about India. While the writings of the ambassador-historian were lost, valuable portions found their way into the manuscripts of the prominent Greek geographer-philosopher-historian Strabo, and this priceless heritage is available to us. Through him we know what the most important part of India, the rich Ganges Valley, looked like before Asoka's time.

Chandragupta had some of the traits of Alexander the Great—a strong personality, quick intelligence, administrative ability, and boldness. He also had some characteristics that were particularly needed in the Orient. He lived like a king "to the purple born," a godlike creature, in the belief that the more divine he appeared the less people would dare to lay their hands on his sacred person. Who would dare to kill a god?

The king surrounded himself with pomp, too, because of his belief that his subjects had to be impressed. But, at the same time, he stood ready to serve his people. The Greek ambassador gave a graphic description of the king's own palace, in the midst of a walled-in park, filled with exotic birds and ornamental trees. The mansion was plated with silver and gold, supplied with huge basins and goblets, some measuring six feet. The residence was further adorned with richly carved tables, sumptuous chairs of state, and Indian copper vessels set with precious gems.

In public, the king was carried on a gold-encrusted palanquin, ornamented with tassels of pearls. On short journeys, he rode on one of his stately steeds. For longer trips he mounted a huge elephant with golden trappings. At all times he was clothed in rich muslin, embroidered with threads of purple and gold.

Entertainments of all kinds were prominent features of court life. The king and his entourage liked to watch the fights of trained elephants, bulls, and rams. Even some rhinoceros could be trained for such feuds. Popular, too, were the ox races, covering distances of six thousand yards. In the carriage races the vehicles were drawn by mixed teams—the horses in the middle and an ox on each side.

The most magnificent royal sport was hunting, accompanied by a ritual. The game was driven toward the elevated platform which the king occupied in an enclosed preserve. The ruler's bodyguards at these hunts were women—amazons—heavily armed and imported from foreign countries beyond the mountain range. They saw to it that outsiders did not approach the king. Those that did were slain.

The amazons also protected him in the interior of the royal residence. His subjects expected the king to show himself to them once a day, to receive petitions, to try court cases, and to offer animal sacrifices to the gods. A curious custom of the king was observed by the

Greek ambassador-historian. While judging cases the king had himself massaged by four attendants. He was not a man to waste his time.

Learning from the example of his predecessor, Chandragupta was careful how he treated philosophers. He was also careful of what he ate. The slaves that cooked his food tasted it in his presence. A network of spies kept him informed of "whispers" in the land. Those suspected of harboring designs on him vanished without a trace. Every night the king changed his sleeping couch, and he did not dare to take a nap during the day. Still, there was always the danger of his being trapped, as indicated by a play about him, which said:

> The brave men who were concealed
> In the subterranean avenue that led
> To Chandragupta's sleeping quarters—thence
> To steal by night and kill him as he slept.

Whatever the royal eccentricities, Magadha was not doing badly under his rule—certainly not in comparison with other lands. Whenever the monsoon rains delivered their celestial gift, the people had enough to eat. The handicrafts of the skilled artisans found ready markets. The Greek ambassador was astounded to see that honesty was so widespread that neither the houses nor the workshops had to be bolted at night. The men of the realm enjoyed the reputation of being uncommonly courageous. However, since the country's frontiers remained secure, they had few occasions to display their martial zeal. The women of the kingdom were known for their chastity. The condition of the slaves was tolerable, and there were only seven castes, as against many hundreds in later times. The relations among members of the occupational groups and castes were good. Both men and women managed to keep sober.

Hinduism, also known as Brahmanism, was the creed of most of the people of the kingdom. It governed their way of life, affecting their daily chores, and was thus more than a religion. Some of the people were followers of Jainism, an offshoot of Hinduism, and Chandragupta may have been one of them. Still others embraced Buddhism, the creed which Asoka was to espouse. And the India of that day, or, for that matter, of today, cannot be understood without knowing about Hinduism, the way of life of the majority.

3

✒ FORTY *CRORES* OF GODS

HINDUISM, the basic creed of India, had great impact upon the life of the Indian people. In the Hindu religion there are forty *crores* of gods. One *crore* is the equivalent of ten million. Therefore, the Hindus have four hundred million gods.

These gods represent countless manifestations of nature—life forces, friendly and hostile, angelic and diabolic. There are special gods of villages, of unusual phenomena of nature in the thick jungles, on the mountain peaks, along the rivers—everywhere.

Hinduism is not a religion in the same sense as the three creeds with which the Western world is mainly familiar: Judaism, the oldest of the monotheistic (belief in one god) religions; Christianity, which has made its greatest conquests in the Western world; and Islam, the youngest of the creeds whose followers believe in one god as creator of the world. The immense number of gods in Hinduism makes it possible for the believer to tailor his own concept of religion to suit his own needs. Still, Hinduism does contain some basic beliefs.

One of these is *samsara*—transmigration of the soul. According to this belief, with one important exception, life never ends. When a living creature is said to die, what actually occurs is a transformation from one life to another. For instance, a prince in this life may, after his "death," become a pauper in his next reincarnation. Or he may become an animal—perhaps a snake. And so on, as life continues through numerous, endless reincarnations.

Who becomes the prince and who becomes the snake in the new life? That depends upon the individuals' deeds—*karma*—good or bad. Good deeds are rewarded and bad deeds are punished in reincarnations. But people have noted throughout the ages that often good people have had bad lives, and bad people have had good lives. That is not cause for concern, Hinduism says, for virtue will be rewarded in future reincarnations. Therefore, it pays to be good in the present life.

The Hindus realized that lifetime sufferings were many and pleasures few. The pauper who becomes a king in the next reincarnation may still be afflicted with many pains. King Chandragupta was such a man. Even though the potentate of the mightiest empire, he did not dare to sleep in the same room two nights in a row. He was constantly in fear of his life. And that was the "best" type of life in his age.

The one exception to endless reincarnations is the greatest reward for virtue. It is not, says Hinduism, the kingly status but the absolute end of all reincarnations, the complete dulling of the senses. In that case, of course, one would feel no pleasure, but no pain either. This absolute end is called the *nirvana*—the blowing out of all life. The word actually does mean "blowing out" in Sanskrit, the classical language of India.

Dharma, which was to play a most important role in Asoka's life, is another basic Hindu doctrine. It means the fulfillment of one's duty to the family, community, and caste (station in life) —the supreme ethical principle, the call of morality and natural law. In certain interpretations of the Hindu creed, it may mean the performance of one's duty to all humanity.

Morality in the highest degree is practiced by ascetics who mortify the body and gratify the soul. The Hindu world abounds in holy men, and the teacher, or *guru*, is given high esteem because he nurtures the soul.

Many things are venerated in the Hindu creed. The cow is not just a household animal, but the symbol of fertility, of the principle of life. It is an ungodly, and even criminal, act to slaughter a cow. Rivers are venerated, too, especially the Ganges. They are not merely symbols of life, but are life itself, awakening nature's slumbering forces in the soil. Without water, the soil becomes death-dealing instead of life-giving. The sins of the faithful followers of the gods can be washed away in consecrated waters, particularly at venerated locations and at auspicious moments.

Hindu life includes the caste system. At first it may have been a way for the conquerors from the north to impose their will and keep the native people under their control. It may also have served at first as mutual assistance associations for members of the same occupations against the encroachments of the people on top.

Countless castes and subcastes have come into being during the course of centuries. Topping them all are the Brahmans (*brah* -mans), the priestly caste. It has been many Indians' great pride that Brahmans—the thinkers and philosophers—have ranked over the warriors.

The Kshatriyas (*kshat* -tre-yas), the warriors, form the second caste, and are called upon to defend their land if need be. This caste was also supposed to provide the rulers of India.

Husbandmen, artisans, merchants, people providing a livelihood for themselves and others, make up the caste of the Vaisyas (*vise* -yas), third in rank, although— many people agree—first in importance. The country could sustain itself without the priests and soldiers, but it could not live without food.

When male members of these three castes reach the age of puberty they undergo initiation rites. According to the Hindus, they are "born again" after the performance of the rite and are, therefore, called *dvija*, twice-born.

Performing the duties of menials and household servants are the Sudras (*soo*-dras), members of the fourth caste, born only once in one earthly life.

The traditional explanation of the origins of the castes indicates their status in the Hindu world. Brahma was the original living force. The Brahmans came out of his mouth—oracles, sages, priests; the Kshatriyas from his arms—men of valor and tribal chiefs; the Vaisyas from Brahma's thighs—strong, muscular, made to perform hard work; and finally, the Sudras from his feet, the lowest and lowliest part of Brahma's body.

When invaders from the north overran India thousands of years ago, they turned some of the population into slaves, forcing them to do lowly chores. These people were made to perform tasks the conquerors considered polluting, such as removing filth and handling skins and hides. The workers were not admitted into the castes, and so were called "outcastes," or "pariahs," a word in Tamil, a language of the defeated natives, meaning "drummer." No caste Hindu would touch a drum made of animal hide because it was considered defiling.

In the course of time, countless subcastes emerged within the castes. They were accompanied by all sorts of restrictions, such as who could marry whom, who could eat with whom without being "defiled" and, therefore, forced to perform acts of purification. Thus came into existence the Indian prohibitions of "intermarriage" and "interdining," which made life more restrictive and complex than before. These restrictions have been plaguing India throughout the ages.

But even worse was the condition of the untouchables. Their very touch was considered defiling, and called for purification rites by higher castes to pacify the gods whose rules had been flouted. One would expect that as children of the same misfortune, the untouchables at least would have pulled together, all victims of the same discrimination of caste. That, however, was not the case. The equivalents of subcastes even came into existence within the pariah ranks. The "superior outcaste" would have nothing to do with the "inferior" ones. Those untouchables who, for instance, were the laundrymen for other outcastes were shunned by their own fellows in misfortune. They were not even allowed to show their faces during the day. Shunning daylight, they became nocturnal creatures who dared to move around only under the cover of darkness.

With all their myriad castes and subcastes, what common bond held the Hindus together? The strongest tie was their sacred books. These books are different from those of the West—the Bible for Christians and Jews; the Koran for Muslims. The western books contain a philosophy of life, commandments, and ethical principles, but the Hindu sacred books are epic stories of high adventure and heroic deeds. They may be philosophical speculations, poems, and occasional admonitions to right conduct.

The *Vedas* were composed over a considerable period of time about a thousand years before Christ. They consist mainly of devotional poems and, thus, come closest to what the West means by sacred writ.

Some time later, presumably in the eighth and seventh centuries before the beginning of the Christian era, the *Upanishads* were written. They are meditative philosophical speculations in verse and prose, seeking to inculcate the love of truth. One of the Upanishads' famous sayings is: "Truth conquers ever; falsehood never."

Another and oft-quoted statement is: "From darkness lead me to light. And from death to immortality!"

The great and much-admired Hindu epic, *Ramayana*, is perhaps twenty-five centuries old. It tells a complex and highly romantic story of the noble Rama who was deprived of his throne by court intrigues. To make matters worse, Ravana, the demon, abducted the hero's wife, Sita. Aided by the monkey general, Hanuman, Rama eventually found his wife. Rama and Sita came to be worshiped as divine personifications. Allegedly, this magnificent epic was written by a former highwayman named Valmiki, who had a change of heart when he saw a dove killed by an arrow. The author of the epic died as a saint.

Another great epic poem, which is a link among the Hindu Indians, is the *Mahabharata*, composed by many bards over a span of several centuries beginning in the fourth century B.C. The main story deals with a dynastic feud within the kingdom of Hastinapur. The most popular part of this classic is the *Bhagavad-Gita*, a summary of the main tenets of Hinduism, which has been compared with the Christian Sermon on the Mount. On the eve of the crucial battle between feuding sections, the divine Lord Krishna and the warrior Arjuna have a talk, in the course of which Krishna reveals that dedicated action, intellectual effort, and devotion to divinity are the paths that lead to salvation and to the triumph of truth.

Hinduism was, as now, the leading religion of India at the time of Chandragupta. The two main reform movements—Buddhism and Jainism—were already several generations old. Jains may be seen, even today, walking with brooms in hand, sweeping the sidewalks on which they tread, in order not to crush even insects, and thus extinguish life. Many of them cover their lips with veils, so as not to inhale and kill gnats. Jains are known in India for their cleanliness, but if they did have parasites feeding on their bodies they would not kill them. All life is sacred to the followers of this sect.

Not only are the Jains forbidden to kill anybody or anything; they are never to tell a falsehood, to steal, or indulge in sexual pleasures. They are supposed to renounce all panderings of their senses. Their "five virtues" are to be acquired with the aid of what the Jains call the three jewels—*triratna*—knowledge, faith, and virtue. With their aid, too, one acquires mastery over the hostile forces of nature. "Man! Thou art thine own friend," the Jains say. "Why lookest thou for a friend beyond thyself?"

It is assumed that King Chandragupta became a Jain, but he does not seem to have learned the substance of his new faith: "Thou shalt not kill." He waged wars—not one, but many. Probably he believed that they were wars of defense and of liberation, and, therefore, justified.

The important achievements of Chandragupta's reign were that he expelled the Greeks from the Punjab, humbled Seleucus the Conqueror, established himself as undisputed lord of northern India and distant lands toward the setting sun, and that he joined the Jain sect of Hinduism. These achievements "entitle him to rank among the greatest and most successful kings known to history," Indian historians say. "A realm so vast and various as his was not to be governed by weakness. The strong hand which won the empire was needed to keep it. . . ." And Chandragupta's hands were strong.

His later years are obscured by few facts and many fancies. He lived more than twenty-three centuries ago, and the land of the Ganges has been ravaged many times throughout those centuries with most of its records lost.

According to one tale, Chandragupta relinquished his throne, the protection of his magnificent amazons, and the adulation of the people. Why would he do that? Perhaps he was tired of sleeping every night in a different bed to trick potential killers. He became a recluse and retired into a forest retreat in the southland. As a hermit he was seeking "illumination," linked to the happy numbness that heralded the ultimate end—*nirvana*. It was not unusual in those days for Jains to seek light while completely neglecting their bodies, neglecting them to the extent of not eating any food, and thus starving themselves to death. Chandragupta may have starved himself to death, too, in his forest retreat. He died in 298 B.C. He had ruled for twenty-four years and his reign was part of a heroic age of India.

Chandragupta's son, Bindusara, now acceded to the
throne, as the ruler whom history knows as Amitraghata,
Slayer of Foes. From this it is assumed that he was not
a Jain as his father had been. Had he been of that sect,
he would not have boasted of killing—not even when the
victims were his foes.

Bindusara is remembered mainly because of a trivial
incident in his life that showed him as a man craving not
only earthly pleasures but also those of the mind. One
day he wrote to the ruler of the realm to the West,
Antiochus Soter (successor of Seleucus Nicator), asking
him to send him three items: sweet wine, figs, and a
Greek philosopher. Back came two of the requested
items: sweet wine and figs. But there was no philosopher
in the shipment. "Men of learning are not for sale in
our land," wrote Antiochus.

Bindusara protected the vast land that he had in-
herited from his father, but he did not measure up to
the greatness of the founder of the Maurya dynasty.

He had sixteen wives who gave him, according to
tradition, about a hundred sons. Daughters were not
considered important enough to be counted. One of
his wives was named Subhadrangi—of Comely Mien—
a Brahman from the province of Bihar. She was also
known by the name of Dharma, or the Righteous One.
This wife presented King Bindusara with two sons,
Tishya and Asoka.

4

⁂ ASOKA WAS JOY

He was born in 291 b.c., or perhaps in 292, or 304. All dates from that era are tentative. He was given the name of Asoka—which means "joy," or "without sorrow." *Asoka-Vardhana*, or Increasing Joy, was another name under which he became known. The place of his birth is not certain either. It was probably the royal capital, Pataliputra.

Asoka was not King Bindusara's eldest son. That was Susima, or Sumana, who played no role in history. The eldest son may not have been in favor with his royal father or may have been incompetent. Or it may have been Asoka's special fitness for the role that earned him the rank and title of crown prince.

We know about Asoka's education—as about the training of other princes—from a notable book, *Arthasatra*, by the same angry Brahman sage, Kautalya, who had helped the Mauryas reclaim their throne. Besides the description of princely education, the book also deals with the art of government.

Children, it is said in the book, matured early in those days. By the age of eight they were at home with the three R's of reading, writing, and arithmetic, and ready to explore such complex problems as those of philosophy. In those days Indian philosophy concerned itself mainly with insights derived from Hindu classics.

The core of Hindu philosophy—dharma—was identical with that of religion, and it was of supreme importance to Asoka throughout his career. Morality, we have seen, was the very substance of dharma, linked to the duties of all men. It saw life as a boon that had to be justified by fulfilling certain obligations imposed on all human beings. First and foremost was the obligation to the nucleus of society, the family. Beyond that, one was in duty bound to the clan and tribe, the beginnings of what today we call the nation. These obligations had to be discharged in noble deeds, by being helpful to others, and promoting the weal of the family, the clan, the tribe. At the end one was to ask: "What have I done to make this a better world?" But . . . there was really no end, because there was no complete extinction of life. On the contrary, there was an endless sequence of lives in the form of reincarnation. Of course, there was nirvana for the highest virtue, but that was a rare exception.

The princely child was also initiated into the art of government—*artha*—which, curiously, also means prosperity. A more abundant life was created with the art of government. The people of India had to be practical-minded if they were to survive. Especially practical-minded were the Mauryas, who anticipated the way of thinking of the American Puritans by more than two thousand years. To them, too, as to the Puritans, prosperity was the reward of virtue. The gods showered their blessings on those who worked hardest. Affluence was a sign of divine blessing.

Another feature of the philosophy imbibed by the princely child was the concern with *danda*, punishment. So important was it that *dandanity* has been translated as the "art of politics." Danda was meted out to the domestic evil-doers and to the enemy from the outside. It was tempered, however, by dharma, and was to be neither capricious nor excessive. The opposite of punishment was embraced by the concept of reward for virtue.

Work alternated with play in the life of the princeling —manly work and manly play. The curriculum included sports, games, and hunting. There was no lack of game in the foothill jungles. In the vast delta of the Ganges and its sister river, the Brahmaputra, the prince could satisfy his fancy for bird hunting. As a youngster, Asoka was bold to the point of recklessness in chariot races. The king's attention to his son's special gifts may have been aroused by his feats in sports.

Life at the court had other notable features, too, and one of these affected Asoka's life. There were festive

gatherings, called *samajas*, which required the slaughtering of countless animals, accompanied by the shedding
of much blood. Asoka was repelled by the sight, and he
was to recall these animal holocausts in years to come.

Bindusara's country was very large, including the most
fertile parts of India. These territories contained all
manner of people with all ways of life. Statesmanship
and craft were needed to keep the restive dwellers of
outlying areas under control. Often the king had to be
represented by viceroys of royal blood. Asoka's practical
education as a ruling prince began when he was still a
teen-ager. His father appointed him, successively, as
viceroy in two important distant areas centering around
Taxila and Ujjain.

The latter was one of the seven sacred cities, a pilgrimage center and trade hub. It appears to have been the
site of Asoka's first tour of duty. Its location was rendered
more important by the fact that it lay along the principal
road from the harbors of the western coast into the interior. Because of its importance it became the head-
quarters of Indian astronomy. As the meridians are
reckoned today from Greenwich, England, so they were
then computed from the longitude of Ujjain in India.

A good location was fine for a major market, but also
an attraction for *dacoits*—bandits—working separately
and in teams. As the viceroy of this region, young Asoka
had to face these ruthless men. He managed to restrain
them, thus earning his royal father's praise. Heeding the
instructions of his childhood teachers, he practiced the

ruler's art of mixing danda with dharma in the correct proportion—condign punishment with broad-minded justice.

The thought of marriage does not seem to have entered Asoka's mind for a long time. He was past the best marriage age, according to the then prevailing Indian custom. Boys of ten were often "seasoned married men," who may have been wedded for years. Most of the boys got married before fifteen. Asoka was already eighteen. Perhaps he had no time to spend with women, or perhaps, being away from home, he spent too much time with them. Possibly, he did not want to be tied down to a restricted life.

Suddenly, at the age of nineteen, he changed his mind. He had set eyes on *the* girl—the only one who appealed to him. She became his wife, the first one.

Her name was Vedisa-Mahadevi-Sakyakumari. The third part of her name identified her background, indicating that her clan was from the Sakya land. It was also the clan of Gautama, the founder of the Buddhist creed. The young wife appears to have been a follower of Lord Buddha and it may have been through her that Asoka had his first contact with the religion.

His work in Ujjain completed, Prince Asoka received another assignment, no less difficult than the previous one. This time he received the vice-regency in Taxila (Takshasila), capital of the northwest, which included Kashmir, the verdant land in the mountains, the dusty Punjab, and the huge provinces of Magadha west of the

Indus River. Today some of this area is situated in the "western wing" of Pakistan, with its famous cities of Rawalpindi and Peshawar. Then, as throughout much of history, part of this area—the Northwest Frontier—was the ruggedly turbulent region of independent-minded mountaineer tribesmen whose restless ways caused endless trouble to their neighbors.

Before the Maurya conquest, parts of this region had been free tribal areas with some strange customs. For instance, a maiden who failed to get a husband before she became too "old" for marriage at fifteen was usually offered for sale by her parents on market days. And another: the bodies of the dead were not buried as Hindu rites required, but were left in the open to be devoured by vultures. The Parsees of India, a small but important sect, still practice this custom today.

Just like Asoka's previous post, Taxila, too, was situated along a major travel artery, the principal highway from the northern mountains to the highlands of the interior, crossing areas rich not only in fertile soil but also in precious stones. Because of its natural wealth, the region needed special care, which it seems to have received under Prince Asoka's rule.

Taxila was the westernmost important Indian city, which enabled Asoka to maintain contact with the Western world in Europe. Under his administration the city became a center of learning. People went there to study medicine, sciences, and the arts. Taxila reminded the prince again of the statesmanlike view of Alexander the

Great, that peace could be best safeguarded by creating a complete global unit, its frontiers strongly entrenched.

Asoka traveled a good deal in his domains and learned a lot about his subjects' lives. He saw the enormously rich people at the top, living like kings on their large estates, fattening on the traders that crossed their realms. Taxila also had its merchant kings, always on the lookout for unusual merchandise, buying and selling at high profits, and amassing great wealth.

The prince was fascinated by the bazaars, the meeting place of artisans, itinerant vendors, acrobats and all kinds of entertainers, drifters, and beggars, too. Swarming with people, the bazaars were exciting and noisy places. Noise was life and it made people stir with excitement.

Yet, death was never distant, and Asoka could not help seeing the corpses filling the lanes after the rains of the season had failed. At those times there was also a large increase in the number of beggars crying for fistfuls of food, without which they faced death.

Although these sights displeased the prince, they did not rob him of his sleep. He had been brought up in the belief that dharma controlled life and death. If people died of starvation, it happened because that was the will of the gods. Besides, they may have committed serious crimes in their previous lives, and now the price had to be paid.

Asoka shared the belief that people dying of starvation were a different breed of men, and not part of the world of a prince such as he. It was the task of the lowly estates to serve members of the higher classes. These, in turn, benefited from the radiance of the gods—darshan. They were the end, and not the beginning, as were the people of common clay. At his early age Prince Asoka was no different in his beliefs from other young princely people of his age and place.

5

✵ A RULER OF GRACIOUS MIEN

Asoka's work at Taxila was completed after a time. He had maintained order and had kept the province quiet. What was to be the next step for him?

There is no portrait of Asoka at this, or any other, time. We can only guess what he looked like. Because of the manly sports he engaged in, his outdoor life, and the rich food he ate, he was probably taller than the average Indian. He must have been conscious of his superior breeding, and that gave him the self-confidence which made him sit proudly erect on his thoroughbred steed. He was a young man of action and—we shall see —also a thinker. A mixture of Gangetic plain dwellers and of highlanders, his skin was probably bronzed and tawny. His hair was smooth and so black that it looked a shade of blue.

It is said that the young prince was not handsome. He liked to think of himself as handsome in later years, when he referred to himself as Piyadasi—of Gracious Mien. But we also have the views of some court ladies, who found him homely.

Asoka's father, King Bindusara, died in 274 or 273 B.C. What happened after his death is a matter of many legends and much speculation. While Asoka was not the eldest son, it was he who ascended the throne. But it took another four or five years before his coronation, which occurred in 269 B.C.

In the intervening period Asoka acted like a monster, according to one legendary account. It originated among people who admired him, the Buddhist monks on the island of Ceylon. A large island off the southernmost tip of India, Ceylon is an independent country today.

Why should admirers depict young Asoka as a monster? That is part of the strange story of how Asoka the Monster became Asoka the Great. The legends perpetuated by the Buddhist monks were meant to build up a sharp contrast. Asoka was evil before his conversion, and an angel afterward. He was converted from Hinduism or Brahmanism, the dominant creed of India, to Buddhism, which he was to embrace and spread all over the known world.

According to the Ceylon legend, Asoka waded to his

throne in the blood of his "hundred brothers." That number arouses suspicion in the first place. There is no reliable record of the number of Asoka's brothers. There is a record, however, that he employed some of his brothers as governors of provinces, especially in Ujjain and Taxila, the same way that he had been employed by his father. There is also a record of one brother who wanted no part in the government of the country, preferring to lead a hermit's life. Asoka not only yielded to his wish, but had a hermitage built for him. There was also a wayward brother whose dissolute ways displeased the king. This brother was a royal deputy who oppressed his subjects, exacting extra tribute to cover the cost of his expensive life. Asoka took his brother to task, telling him that his ways were embarrassing to the royal rule. The brother was so impressed by the king's concern that, after having confessed his failings, and manifesting repentance, he expressed his readiness to withdraw to a hermitage.

"The bloodbath of the hundred" is certainly not based on fact. Modern scholarship accepts the view that Asoka succeeded his father peaceably, in accordance with Bindusara's wish. There is a possibility, however, according to the authoritative study, *The Early History of India*, by Vincent A. Smith, that the Indian "northern tradition which testifies to a contest for the succession between Asoka and Susima, his eldest brother, may be founded on fact." This may explain the time lag between Asoka's accession to the throne and his coronation. The

northern tradition of feud between the two brothers
sounds far more authentic than the stories perpetuated
by the Ceylon monks.

Another of the Ceylon legends attributes a particularly
monstrous act to Asoka before his conversion.

A large group of high-spirited young ladies-in-waiting
at the court were romping about in the royal garden of
Pataliputra, the capital. There were five hundred of
them, according to the story—a suspiciously large number again. In the garden stood a tree that was particularly
dear to the king. It was dedicated to Kama, the goddess
of love. The official name of the tree was *Saraca Indica*,
unofficially known as *Asoka*—Joy. In their unrestrained
play, the young women broke off branches of the tree,
while making loud references to the king's unattractive
looks. It was their misfortune that Asoka overheard them.
His wrath knew no bounds, according to the legend,
and he called in those of his servants who were notorious
for their brutality. Promptly, the king issued orders that
all of the five hundred young women should be burned
alive.

There was no atrocity that the Ceylon story-tellers
did not impute to Asoka, but always before his conversion to Buddhism. They concocted the legend of a
"royal pleasure lodge" to make him appear even more
of a monster. The lodge was erected in the royal capital
and looked very pleasant, indeed, on the outside. Some
people, such as the enemies of the king, were invited
to enjoy his hospitality in this lovely house. They entered
it and found inside a raging hell, in which they were

subjected to excruciating tortures. Who they were no-body knew for sure, because nobody left the "pleasure house" alive. But there was one exception, as absurd, according to the legend, as the other stories of Asoka's misdeeds.

One of the "guests" in the house of torture was an ascetic who had dared to criticize the king's evil deeds. His name was Balapandita, and he was a saintly man. Invited into the "pleasure house," he was to be given the usual treatment. Royal henchmen put him in a huge caldron placed upon an open fire. The executioners left him alone to face an agonizing death. After a while they returned to collect the remains of the victim. In-stead, they saw the ascetic sitting quietly atop a huge lotus flower, unscathed and engaged in meditation.

Then Asoka was converted to Buddhism. Suddenly, all the fires of hell surrounding the royal residence were extinguished, and celestial peace invaded Asoka's world. The most evil of the evil now turned into the purest of the pure. The extremes of public relations, familiar to us today, were evidently known thousands of years ago on the Buddhist island of Ceylon.

The legends now changed to show "Asoka the Angel." At the time of this story Asoka no longer lived with his first wife, Mahadevi. His son by that marriage was Kunala, a good and faithful child, devoted to his father. Asoka now had several chief wives, one of whom was Tisiaraksyta, a thoroughly evil woman. (Only step-mothers in Ceylonese legends can be as evil as she was.)

Although Kunala was very young, he was already

married, as was customary in India. The stepmother
became infatuated with the youth and wanted him to
return her affections. But Kunala was a loyal son and a
faithful husband. Rebuffed, Tisiaraksyta swore ven-
geance. Finally, she thought, her moment came.

Asoka evidently trusted his son's common sense, and
he appointed him to the same post he had once occupied
in Taxila. He gave strict instructions to Kunala always
to verify the orders that he received from the king. The
country was large and its bureaucracy complicated, and,
evidently, there were cases of fraud in the transmission of
royal decrees. The king hit upon an ingenious device in
his instructions to his son. Every royal order had to
have Asoka's seal, which bore the imprint of his front
teeth. The son had a sample of the seal for verification.

Kunala performed his tasks to the satisfaction of the
king, but not of his stepmother. Still nursing her grudge,
she worked out a device to destroy the young man
through his eyes, the feature she admired most. She drew
up an order in the name of the king, addressed to Asoka's
ministers in Taxila, and instructed them to gouge out
Kunala's eyes. To make the order authentic, she had to
obtain the imprint of the royal teeth, and that was not
easy. Fired by the insane wish to perform this evil act,
the king's chief wife prepared a sleeping potion, which
put Asoka into a torporlike sleep. Thus, she obtained
the authentication of the order which she promptly dispatched to the ministers in Taxila.

The ministers were speechless upon receipt of the
royal order. Could there have been an error, and what

were they to do? They decided to request a confirmation in the capital. Meanwhile, they had the prince detained. Kunala noted that something was amiss, and he demanded an explanation. The ministers could not help telling him of his father's instructions. The son compared the imprint of the teeth on the order and on the sample seal he carried. There was no question of the authenticity of the royal will. Kunala told the ministers that the order had to be executed without any delay, but they demurred. Kunala insisted. But they could find nobody in the entire town to carry out the monstrous deed. Finally, Kunala himself found a person to execute the order for a fee, and his eyes were plucked out.

Kunala had no money, nor did he accept funds from the ministers. He and his young wife left the viceregal palace with no earthly belongings, except begging bowls for food. The young couple wandered all over the land. One day they reached the royal residence city, and took themselves into the courtyard of the palace.

The princely beggars had discovered that they had a better chance of getting food if they sang songs, and they had also acquired lutes in their wanderings. Plucking the strings of their musical instruments, the couple sang a song of sadness and despair. "What pain we have to suffer, alas, from hunger and cold." Then Kunala continued: "Once I was a prince and now I am a beggar. Would that I could make myself known and gain redress."

In his chambers, the king heard the plaint and found the singer's voice familiar. He sent for the minstrel,

who presented himself with his young wife. Beholding
his son, the king was thunderstruck. Moved to tears, he
wanted to know how this tragedy had been brought
about. He learned that the ministers' query about the
confirmation of his order had been intercepted by his
wife. Although he would punish the evil woman, what
was he going to do for his son?

Being in a state of grace—after his conversion—Asoka
had a moment of illumination. He thought of a saintly
man by the name of Ghosha, living in a Buddhist
monastery near the holy tree called Mahanbody. The
saintly man might be able to help the prince.

The Buddhist sage acted promptly. He invited his
disciples for a meeting of meditation and self-purifica-
tion, and he also asked them to bring along vessels for
the collection of human tears.

At the appointed time, the followers were assembled,
including King Asoka, Kunala, and his young wife. The
saintly man delivered a homily, telling the story of
Kunala's blinding, which he related to the performance
of one's duty—dharma—and how the loyal son insisted
on following his father's instructions even in the face of
the ministers' doubt. As he spoke, not one eye in the
entire assembly remained dry, and the vessels became
filled with tears, which the saintly Ghosha collected.
Then he said to his disciples:

"I have told you the story of Kunala and also ex-
pounded to you the teachings of Lord Buddha. If there
were errors in my words, let matters stand as they are
now. But if I have committed no errors, let this young
man regain his sight."

Then the sage washed Kunala's eyes with the tears, while the audience watched. Miraculously, the prince regained his eyesight. The assemblage shouted the praises of the king and prince, and everyone was overjoyed. Thus, virtue was rewarded.

As we know, there was a span of some four years between Asoka's assumption of power and his coronation. What accounts for this delay? There may have been challengers to his succession (as with his brother), and there may also have been a civil war. In the course of those years, the challengers must have been rebuffed, but the records shed no light on this period.

The coronation—*abhisheka*—seems to have taken place in 269 B.C. The ceremony was filled with tradition and symbols. The center of the highly elevated stage was occupied by a magnificent throne, representing the supreme authority. The throne was covered with the skin of a leopard, the symbol of strength. Facing the high nobility and the chiefs of the clans, Asoka stood on the lower steps of the staircase leading to the throne, inviting the chiefs to ascend, an invitation that was not to be taken literally.

Brahmans from Kashmir, India's loftiest region, performed the rite, because their land was closest to the dwellings of the gods. They had collected holy water from the seas surrounding India, and now sprinkled it on the prince. Through this ritual, the mortal became immortal, the human turned into superhuman, and the common clay was changed into the substance of divinity.

The ceremony of the coronation over, the new king performed many charitable acts: he commuted death sentences and released prisoners from jails. Then followed the festivities that both the nobility and the common people were to remember all their lives, including the royal repast with a generous distribution of food to the poor. Next came the display of many manly arts, especially wrestling, archery, and chariot races. With the end of the ceremony, the Age of Asoka began.

The years that followed were not at first distinguished by any noteworthy act, although King Asoka seems to have been an effective ruler. Taxes were collected, as always, and order of a sort was maintained. The rich were very rich; the poor very poor. The people ate their fill when the gods were gracious and when heaven discharged its blessings in the form of the monsoon during the rainy season. When there was no such blessing, there was death in the land.

There was death also because of border wars. Asoka's land was the richest part of India, watered by the blessed Ganges. It was also blessed by the forty *crores*—four hundred million—gods. But then came the Kalinga War, which changed the life of Asoka, and also the future of India. It helped the king to become Asoka the Great. The mortal now really became immortal. Out of hundreds of Indian rulers in the course of generations, only the name of Asoka still shines.

The Bay of Bengal flanks India in the east. Between two major rivers—Mahanadi and Godawari—was a long strip of land called Kalinga. In the thirteenth year of Asoka's reign, and nine years after his coronation, he engaged in the Kalinga War. There was nothing unusual about a war then, as there is still nothing unusual about wars now. But the Kalinga War turned out to be different.

There may have been one or more reasons for waging this war. Kalinga was adjacent to Magadha, and its people may have been Asoka's tributaries. They may have failed to deliver the annual tribute, and so there was war. Or Asoka may have started the campaign for other reasons—glory or riches, or for an opportunty to provide work for more people in his kingdom. The tribes of Kalinga may have rebelled against Asoka's tribute collectors. Or Asoka may have waged a war to extend his domains to more favorable boundaries, having the example of Alexander the Great in mind. He may have launched the war to divert attention from persistent problems at home—a customary procedure then as now. It is also possible that the war may have been started not by Asoka but by one or more Kalinga chiefs, for prestige, gems, or food.

Whatever the cause, it was a bloody and brutal war. When it was over, Asoka estimated the losses of the enemy at about one hundred thousand killed and many times that number as victims of famine and pestilence. One hundred and fifty thousand of the people of Kalinga were taken captive and dragged into slavery. Women and children were counted among the dead and enslaved.

Because it was a particularly vicious war, blood was shed not merely in the endeavor to defeat the foe, but also for the savage excitement of the battle. The soldiers seemed to love the sight and smell of human blood.

Viewing the dead made the living ecstatic that they were alive. The misfortune of others compensated for the frustrations of their own lives.

Asoka won, and as a result of his victory, he was on the way to becoming the Alexander the Great of India. Indeed, the entire subcontinent was his, except for the extreme south. His kingdom included not only most of the India of today, but also the two wings of Pakistan, the Punjab in the west and Bengal in the east. In the west it extended into the land of the Afghans and parts of Persia. The tallest ranges of the world—Himalayas, Karakorum, and Hindu Kush—protected the kingdom from the unknown dangers to the gloomy north.

"He [Asoka] was now in the mid-peak of his glory," say the historians H. T. and D. L. Thomas. "If he went on, he might attain such heights of conquest as would dwarf even the exploits of Alexander. But Asoka did no such thing. His last victory filled him with the 'sadness of satiety.'"

This was the turning point in the life of Asoka, the parting of the ways. He had been Asoka the Demon, and would now become Asoka the Great. After his victory in the Kalinga War, the king was haunted by one question—Why? Had he really scored a victory? He remembered the piles of corpses and the line of hopeless slaves. Was it really so glorious to kill people and to enslave them? Was it so glorious even though one gained additional land? Was it really glory he had gained? Asoka felt that it was not.

The king carved his repentance into eternal stone,

which can be read even today. He set up thousands of memorial columns after his conversion. One of them, known as the Kalinga Edict, tells about his change of heart:

"After that [the Kalinga War], now that the Land of the Kalingas had been taken, the King is devoted to a zealous study of morality, and to the instruction of morality to the people. This is the repentance of Devan-amprya [favorite of the gods] on account of his conquest of the Kalingas."

As if in a flash, Asoka realized that slaughter was not tantamount to victory, and that only dharma, the law of morality, could achieve conquest through the unity of the human fate. Enough of victory, of slaughter, hatred, and glory. The savage warrior had become converted to the gospel of peace, one of the strangest conversions in the history of the human race. It was strange then, and is strange even today.

What had really brought about Asoka's conversion? In his travels, he had come under the influence of Buddhism, a religious sect that arose in India during the sixth century B.C. At home and abroad Asoka now became the missionary of the teachings of Buddha. He was for Buddhism what Emperor Constantine of the Eastern Roman Empire was to be for Christianity several centuries later. Asoka organized Buddhism as a state religion. No longer did he contrive the destruction of presumed enemies. Instead, he wanted to conquer his baser instincts. He became the apostle of an ethical system, the upholder of an eternal law of morality and piety. It was, mainly, in an attempt to promote the moral principles of Buddha, his immortal master, that Asoka took the steps that have assured him immortality also—those famous memorial columns. Not only was the king a missionary, but he also became an *upasaka*, a lay disciple, dedicated to lead an unblemished life.

Asoka had found the minor sect of Buddhism, an off-shoot and reforming movement of Brahmanism, and turned it into a world religion, such as it is today. At this point his name became intertwined with that of Lord Buddha. Therefore, we must take a close look at the Enlightened One—Buddha—and his immortal creed.

6

✤ THE ENLIGHTENED ONE

"MOST people, Kamala, are like a falling leaf that drifts and turns in the air, flutters and falls to the ground. But a few others are like stars which travel one defined path: no wind reaches them; they have within themselves their guide and path. Among all the wise men, of whom I knew many, there was one who was perfect in this respect. I can never forget him. He is Gautama, the Enlightened One, who preaches his gospel. Thousands of young men hear his teachings every day and follow his instructions every hour, but they are all falling leaves; they have not the wisdom and guide within themselves." So says Siddhartha, as he talks to Kamala, a courtesan, in a novel by Hermann Hesse, the German writer and winner of the Nobel Prize.

The Enlightened One was born with the name of Siddhartha Gautama (or Gotama), about three centuries before Asoka. He is known to the world as the Buddha. Sakyamuni was another of his names—sage of the Sakya tribe from the borderland of Nepal, a small country leaning against the southern Himalayan slope.

The father of Gautama was called Suddhodana, the chieftain, or prince, of a small country about three hundred square miles in size, one of the many tiny principalities in India. The capital was Kapilavastu. Although the country was small, a large retinue catered to the family's whims. This Sakya prince, as the others in the northland, lived in stately mansions in the shade of pipal and banyan trees, in the midst of exotic blooms.

The prince had several wives, two of whom were daughters of the lord Koli, another small tribal area a short distance away. Maha Maya, the older of the two, was forty-five and expecting a child. She wanted her child to see its first day in her father's house, and so she set out in that direction. On the way to the paternal home, she was overwhelmed by weakness, and stopped to rest in a grove along a creek. The grove was called Lumbini, a goddess' name.

The gods, meanwhile, had assembled in their heavenly abode, according to the legend, and Nalaka, the sage, asked why they were together and rejoicing. "Because," he was told, "the Enlightened One, the future Buddha, is about to be born in the Lumbini grove, in Sakya land."

There, indeed, the child was born, as recorded in an ancient ballad: "That wisdom child, that jewel so precious it cannot be matched, was born in Lumbini for mankind's weal and joy."

At the moment of the birth, two streams of water, one warm and one chill, fell from the sky to bathe the mother and the child. The moment after his birth, the child took seven steps toward each of the four quarters of the world and uttered in a loud voice: "I am the master of the world."

Maya reached her father's house and lived there for seven days. Then she ascended to one of the Buddhist heavens.

Superhuman beings—*jins*—brought the good news to the father. He gave his son the name of Siddhartha (or Siddharth) Gautama.

Shortly after the birth, the father summoned the sages of his land to hear their prophecy. He also wanted to hear how to keep Gautama away from harm.

The sages of Sakya country told him: "The young prince will follow in the footsteps of his most illustrious father unless . . . he casts his youthful eyes upon the following—a sorely afflicted man, a decrepit old man, and a corpse. Should that happen, he will renounce his exalted station in life and retire into the forest as a hermit."

Now the father knew what to do. As his son was growing up, the prince had the boy surrounded by young attendants and courtesans to screen out the miseries of life. Never was he to see bodily affliction, old age, or a corpse.

Siddhartha lived the life of a dissolute prince, as, indeed, he was encouraged to do. Finally, the time came for him to get married, and his wife was Yasodhara, daughter of the ruler of the adjacent Koli country.

One day, when the prince was twenty-nine, he went to his usual playgrounds in the company of his charioteer and some companions. There he saw the three forbidden sights—a man wracked by the plague, an old man on the threshold of death, and a corpse.

Siddhartha had seen only smiles and had heard only lovely songs until then. Now he saw the face of death and heard the moaning of hopelessness. Thoroughly shaken, he turned to his charioteer:

"What is this?" he asked.

The charioteer, whose name was Channa, answered boldly, "Behold, this is the fate of man."

He repeated those words a second time.

So this was real life, the young prince discovered, and not the life of luxury he knew. He saw now that he had been kept in an artificial world, removed from reality. Real life must be terrible, filled with pain, and with a premonition of the end.

On the same day Siddhartha Gautama also beheld another sight. He saw a man of dignified bearing, with a sweet and gentle smile.

"Who is this man?" the prince asked Channa eagerly.

"His name I know not," Channa answered. "But I do know that he carries on his lips the words of the gods, that he is an itinerant teacher and an ascetic."

Gautama made no answer and proceeded to the games.

He indulged in the usual manly sports, hardening his body, and deriving much joy from the use of his muscles. Then he took his bath in the stream, feeling refreshed. At the appointed time he ordered his charioteer to drive him home. He entered the paternal house and proceeded to his chambers. There he received the news for which his father's subjects had been waiting—the birth of Gautama's son, his heir and the future ruler, Rahula.

The happy tidings spread quickly, and soon crowds of people began to congregate in front of the princely residence. They cheered themselves hoarse and the new father was obliged to appear before them several times. This was his day of triumph.

Gautama's father, elated by the news, set out to celebrate the happy occasion. He called the best dancing girls and the most accomplished lute-players to entertain. The prince was faced with smiling countenances and he heard melodious sounds. But he could not forget the three terrible sights of the day—the sick, the old, the dead. Nor could he forget the look of quiet happiness on the face of the recluse.

After visiting his wife and child, Gautama took himself to his sleeping chamber. He fell asleep promptly, but when the midnight watch sounded, the prince stirred himself from his slumber.

"Who is on guard?" he wanted to know.

The guard was his charioteer, Channa. Gautama ordered him to saddle a horse.

While this was being done, the prince opened the door of his wife's chamber. She was asleep, one hand resting

lightly on the newborn child. Flowers surrounded them.
He would have liked to enfold his child in his arms and
kiss his wife. But he did not want to rouse them and so
he tore himself away.

The full July moon shone brightly as the young prince
left his father's house, with Channa as his sole com-
panion. He was leaving behind his wife and child, his
wealth, his throne. It was his intention to go into the
wilderness, to become a homeless wanderer, to see life
as it really was, and not as the artificial existence of
smiles. He was going into the forests at first, where there
were few people, to think and think again. Only a small
corner of life had been revealed to him, and yet he saw—
perhaps guessed more than he saw—how much suffering
there was in the life of the common people. He wanted
to know what caused this suffering. He wanted to be a
chela, a student, learning all the time. And after a long
while, he might become a *guru*, a teacher, with that sweet
smile around his lips—the smile that he had seen earlier
on the hermit's face. He would be happy if he could
learn enough to teach others to meet life. Yes, he wanted
the light of knowledge to pierce through the darkness
of his ignorance. Then he would visit his father's house
again, to see his wife and child. Because then he would
feel that his own life had some value.

That night Gautama rode a long distance across his
father's domain, and across the land of Koli. He rode
beyond that, and reached the river Anoma, stopping in
a grove on the riverbank. He cut off his long locks, and
removed his princely ornaments. He handed them to

Channa, instructing him to take them back to the ancestral house. Then he bade the charioteer to go on his way in peace.

Gautama remained alone in the lustrous July night, with no courtly retinues to shield him from reality. His life as a hermit had begun. With a begging bowl he went from village to village, becoming acquainted with real life and with suffering. Now he saw many people afflicted with ailments, and many dead bodies, especially when the monsoon rains had failed. He did not see very many old people, however, for the villagers died young.

In his wanderings, Gautama was learning all the time. More and more people began to take him for a saintly *guru*, and they came to seek his advice. They did not know of his princely background, but something attracted them to him—something, perhaps, in his warm, friendly eyes and his compassionate, melodious voice.

He visited the kingdom of Magadha, ruled by King Bimbisara. The king, having heard of the unusual hermit, invited him to the royal court, hoping to gain enlightenment from his wisdom. But Gautama remained tongue-tied, believing that he still had much to learn.

The hermit continued on his way. Sometimes he could eat his fill, at other times he went hungry. Weakness overcame him one day on the road; he collapsed in a heap and was taken for dead. But he was strong and he recovered.

Another time he saw a vision and heard a voice. It was Mara, goddess of sin, the great tempter, who appeared before him.

"Abandon your project," the tempter said. "Abandon it and a great empire will be yours."

He closed his ears to her.

The evil one pledged revenge: "Lustful thoughts will enter your mind one day and then you will be mine. But the empire, which you could have now, will not be yours."

Six years had passed since Gautama had left the paternal house, and he was now almost ready to give up the search. What did he search for? He sought the light. In his wanderings he reached the town of Gaya, a place of pilgrimage for Hindus. Weary and disheartened, Gautama rested under a bo tree. Legend says that he fasted under the tree for seven days and seven nights, hoping that, free of the trammels of physical existence, the light would come to him. The light would illuminate the answer he sought. He asked to know what caused human suffering, for now he knew that, whether prince or pauper, suffering was everyone's lot.

And under that bo tree the light did come to Gautama, who thenceforth was to be the Buddha—the Enlightened One. Under the tree he began to develop the philosophy which the world would know as Buddhism.

Awareness of suffering was the foundation of his philosophy. "Birth is attended by pain," the Enlightened One learned. "Disease is painful, decay is painful, and painful is the thought of death. Union with the unpleasant is painful, and painful is the separation from the pleasant."

"Behold," Buddha said, "this first Noble Truth."

Now he had to discover the cause of this universal, all-embracing suffering. In that moment of illumination under the bo tree at Gaya he found the cause. The cause of suffering was *tanha*—thirst. It was the thirst for intoxicants, not for the clear water of brooks. Tanha meant to him the desire to amass wealth, fame, and glory for this world, and not for the next. It was the craving to do battle, to overwhelm, to crush and conquer, to win and boast, to strut, to dominate. This Buddha considered the second Noble Truth.

The third Noble Truth was the flaming desire, the lust to quench the thirst for earthly goods. It was the wisdom to cast out the roots of pain, bringing about the end of longing. With that burden removed, one could soar aloft.

The fourth and last Noble Truth was the knowledge of the Eightfold Path—one path in eight, showing the way to life without tanha, the excruciating thirst.

The "right view" was one of the eight paths, the ability to see and to appraise. With the aid of the right view, the disciple had reason to hope that he would reach the path of right aspirations. These were not aspirations for the benefit of self, but for the benefit of the brotherhood, and all men formed part of that.

Leading to the supreme goal—life without ignoble desires—were the remaining six paths: right mindfulness, concentration, effort, speech, conduct, and mode of living. Each path was marked, not by visible signs, but by signs within the seeker. Each path had to be found with the help of a guide—a guide within oneself. No priests were needed nor was an organized church. Membership in the brotherhood was desirable, such as a monastery, or a convent. Another age expressed Buddha's thought in a different language: "Act in such a way that your conduct might become a signpost to all people at all times"—the Golden Rule.

The Buddha was now the Enlightened One, possessing the wisdom to teach prince and pauper about the Noble Truths and the paths leading to them. This was his first advice:

"We are a brotherhood of sufferers—being members of the human race. A living creature is a poem of pity. Suffering is reduced if we form a family—of brothers. We are all brothers in sustaining pain."

There may be an end to suffering, Buddha thought, as the reward of the *arhat*, or holy man, the depository of the highest virtue. For the privileged ones there would be the end of reincarnation, the complete cleansing of the basic wrong, which was the ignoble desire, sensuality. Buddha called that end "the harbor of refuge," "farther shore," "place of bliss," "the home of peace," "holy city," and "the cool cave." It was the house of untroubled slumber, of the blissful numbness; it was nirvana.

The Enlightened One was a product of his age and of his environment, and he had not come into the world to deny his ancestors' faith. He was a Hindu, believing in the basic Hindu views of life and death. He believed that Karma predetermined one's place in later lives. He believed in reincarnation. And he believed in dharma—duty, piety, decent conduct.

Having been born into a world of traditions, Buddha did not lead a movement of reformation. He merely wanted to reinterpret his ancestors' ancient creed. But he did not believe in the forty *crores* of gods, for there was only one God, whose image was engraved in every heart. The name of that God was Truth. Everyone was born with the knowledge of truth, but it had to be found within oneself—an instrument of personal adjustment to each individual life.

Meditation—collective and individual—helped one to find the truth. As a reward for great concentration, there might come the flash of light, such as Buddha's own moment of illumination under the bo tree at Gaya.

Buddha did not criticize any of the four hundred million gods, perhaps because of his ancestral tradition or because all the gods were manifestations of the one God. These may have been the reasons that he did not engage in a war of reformation, nor even feud with the priests. It was not in his nature to wage wars, not even for a just cause, not even for the greatest cause. It was not in his nature, probably, because he knew that truth was the victim of wars.

"Words of doctrine" was the name given to the collection of Buddha's words. The substance of his teaching was contained in the first sermon that he preached after his flash of enlightenment—"Discourse on the Turning of the Wheel of Law." That was the wheel that Asoka used as the symbol of his creed—his spiritual likeness, the eternity of the flow of life, the past, present, and future being sectors of the same reality.

These are some of the Buddha's guidelines:

If one man conquer in battle a thousand times a thousand men, and if another conquer himself, the latter is the greater hero.

By one's-self the evil is done; by one's-self one suffers; by one's-self the evil is undone; by one's-self one is purified. The pure and the impure stand and fall by themselves, and no one can purify another.

The foolish keep on living their futile, indolent, weak, and licentious lives. Theirs is a life of vanity not worth having. . . . And he who lives a hundred years, ignorant and unrestrained, the life of one day is better if a man is wise and thoughtful. . . . And he who lives a hundred years, weak and idle, the life of one day is better if a man has got a firm hold of himself. . . . And he who has learned little, grows old like an ox; his flesh grows but his knowledge does not grow. . . . Rouse theyself, be not idle, and follow the path of virtue.

After some of his followers had formed monasteries, Buddha addressed them:

Rouse thyself by thyself, examine thyself by thy-

7

⚜ THE LIGHT ABLAZE

Hindu traditions acknowledge four stages in the development of the individual. The first is that of the *chela*, apprentice, who imbibes words of the sages and leads a noble life. The second stage is that of the householder, devoted to assiduous life and supporting one's kin. Having provided for his family and having guided his children to maturity, the third stage is reached, that of the *anchoret*. At this stage the passions that sear the soul are shed, and the light that takes one aloft is sought. The fourth stage is finally reached, that of the religious mendicant, who spreads the light and provides sage advice, thus hoping for the higher reincarnation and, possibly, for the supreme bliss of the nirvana.

Gautama, having become the Buddha, stood on the highest stage. He advised his disciples: "I am free now of the hindrances that grip men and the angels, like an immense dragnet. Go now ye, brethren, wander forth for the weal of the many, out of compassion for the world. . . . Preach the doctrine, beauteous in its inception, in its sequel, in its end. Keep on proclaiming the pure and perfect life!"

Buddha founded the system of brotherhoods called *bhikkus*, Buddhist monks who spread the teachings about the sanctity of life, telling people not to speak untruths, not to indulge in immoral life, not to steal another's property, and not to drink intoxicating beverages. The disciples were enjoined to teach the supreme doctrine of *ahimsa*, nonviolence, the creed of forbearance and charity. They encouraged laymen to contribute toward building of monasteries and providing for monks.

Buddha's fame spread far and wide, to his own Sakya clan and to its capital, Kapilavastu. His father, Suddhodana, was now an aged man, and he wished to sit at the feet of the Enlightened One before his death. Buddha, the son, came to his father.

In a grove outside the town, Buddha stopped for the night, and there his father and uncles found him. They were shocked by the sight. He wore no beard and no shoes. His garments were in rags and he looked like a slave. The son was indeed a mendicant with a beggar's bowl. Without asking to sit at his feet, father and uncles returned to town.

The next morning Buddha set out for his father's

capital, carrying his begging bowl and asking for alms.
When the king heard of this, he rushed out of the palace.
The king addressed his son as "Illustrious Buddha,"
and pleaded with him.

"Why doest thou expose us to this shame?" the king
said. "Is it necessary to beg for thy food from door to
door? Doest thou believe that I cannot provide for thy
needs and the needs of thy friends?"

Buddha replied, "My noble father, these are the
customs of our brotherhood."

Suddhodana escorted his son into his mansion and
listened to Buddha's exposition of the creed.

Buddha did not stay long in the ancestral house, for
he scorned being treated as a prince. Soon he resumed
his travels and on his wanderings went again to Pataliputra which, generations later, would be Asoka's home.
Again King Bimbisara invited him and his disciples to
a lavish meal. Buddha told the king that they were used
to the simplest of foods. During the course of the evening, Buddha instructed the assembly.

Bimbisara begged the Enlightened One to stay close
to the court as a teacher, but Buddha replied that his
duty called him to other places. The king then gave
Buddha a bamboo grove on the outskirts of the town,
where he and his disciples could spend the rainy season.
The Enlightened One spent many monsoons in that
grove, preaching inspired sermons. He attracted notable
followers, such as Mogallana and Sariputta, from the
kingdom of Magadha, among the first to enter his
brotherhood.

With fame came offers from prominent people to serve Buddha and his cause, but he accepted only those who wanted to make sacrifices, interviewing the candidates himself. One day a prosperous merchant from Sunaparante called on him, asking to join the order so that he could enlighten his kin. Buddha recalled that on a visit to the merchant's town, he had been badly treated.

He said to the merchant, "The people of Sunaparante are known to be violent in expressing their views. What will you do, if they revile you?"

"If they revile me, I will make no reply."

"And if they strike you?"

"I will not return the blow."

"And if they try to kill you?"

"Death holds no fear for me. Indeed many people crave it so as to escape the vanities of life," said the merchant. "I will take steps neither to delay nor to hasten my end."

Buddha then told him, "You have my permission to teach."

One day during his travels Buddha saw a peasant harvesting his crop. The farmer's acreage was large. With alms bowl in hand, Buddha began to preach to the man, but the farmer interrupted him.

"Why do you come and beg?" he said. "You can see that I sow, I plow, I earn my bread. You should do the same."

To this Buddha replied, "That's what I am doing. I sow, I plow, and then I eat."

"I don't see you sowing and plowing," the farmer answered.

Buddha said, "In my work the seed is the faith, the fertilizing rain is self-restraint. The weeds I destroy are evil desires. The plowing is the knowledge I have acquired, and modesty is the guiding shaft. Perseverance draws my plow which I guide with my mind. The field I labor is that of dharma, the law of morality, and the harvest is nirvana. Sorrow is another type of weed I seek to destroy."

In one village he heard of a distraught young mother whose child had recently died. Her mind clouded because of her bereavement, she went from house to house entreating the neighbors for some magic herb to revive the child. A sympathetic but helpless neighbor sent her to Buddha.

"Lord and master," the young woman asked, "doest thou know of any herb to cure my child?"

"I do, indeed," Buddha promptly replied.

"What is it, master?" she asked.

"It is some mustard seed. Get it for me."

The woman was elated, since mustard seed was an easy herb to find.

"But," Buddha added, "thou shouldst get it from a house where no child, spouse, parent, or slave has died."

The young mother knocked at the door of a hut, asking for the herb. Recalling Buddha's words, she added, "Has a child, spouse, parent, or slave died in this house?"

"Lady, what is it thou askst? The living are few; the dead are many."

She received the same answer in all the huts that she tried. Unable to find a single house without grief, the woman's mind began to clear. When she returned to Buddha, he asked her, "Hast thou brought the mustard seed?"

"My Lord," she replied, "I have not. People tell me the dead are many, the living few."

Then Buddha talked to her about the lot of man, the inevitable suffering, and the need to accept the blows of fate. Quietly, the young mother buried her child and asked to be admitted into Buddha's order, open for nuns as well as for monks.

The years passed; nearly forty-five years since Buddha had first seen the light in the Lumbini grove. Now he was on his way to the land of his birth, in the foothill country of Nepal, to the town of Kusinagara. He was accompanied by his faithful followers, including Ananda, his cousin and closest disciple.

At the grove of Pawa, Buddha felt weakness overwhelm him and he decided to rest. The grove had been presented to the wandering brotherhood by Chuna, the goldsmith, one of the faithful. While resting, Buddha instructed his followers about the need to build more *viharas*, places of retreat, and to concentrate on the Noble Truths and the Eightfold Path.

"Thoughts are wayward, hard to control. On the least slackening of attention, they jump from object to object, like monkeys from branch to branch of trees."

He also recommended an apprenticeship of ten years in higher religious education, of which dharma was to be the pivot. With that, one could also solve everyday problems. He summed up the essence of his teaching in these words: *satyameva Jayate*—nothing is higher than truth.

Buddha enjoined upon his disciples the obligation to master the twenty-five practical virtues. These included, among others, the obligation to familiarize themselves with Buddha's thoughts, born of the enlightenment under the bo tree and of the meditations of many years. The disciples had to learn to apply these thoughts to all situations and to help people who sought their advice. The disciples were told to see people in the light of their own natures, and they had to offer aid without thinking of their own interests.

As Buddha rested in the grove, the faithful goldsmith, Chuna, prepared the evening meal. Refreshed, the small group moved onward, on the final lap of the long trip. They reached the river Kukushta, where Buddha performed his ritual bath. Again he felt vigor returning to him, although he was still weak.

After a while they continued their journey, reaching another stream, the Hiranyavati. There the weary Buddha lay down under a sal tree, his face toward the sun, and he talked about the twenty-five virtues. His voice began to falter and the disciples saw that the end was near. Ananda, unable to restrain his tears, moved out of view, so as not to distress the master. Noting this, Buddha admonished him.

"Weep not, Ananda; recall that this body of ours has the means of renewing its strength only for a limited time. Is there anything put together that will not fall apart, in the end?"

Buddha's presence quickly became known to the neighborhood, and people rushed from the nearby hamlet to set their eyes on him, perhaps for the last time. Among those who came was the philosopher Subhadra, who wanted to know what final advice the Enlightened One could offer.

"Since the age of twenty-nine, O Subhadra," answered Buddha, "I have striven after pure wisdom. Following the right paths I think I have found what I have been seeking all along; the end of all illusions, nirvana. Soon I will be free of earthly bonds."

Then he turned to the grieving disciples.

"Don't think that Buddha will be absent when he passes away. My words will help you to seek the truth. You will have also the by-laws of *samgha*, our order. Take them as your guides."

Having said this, he fell into a comalike trance, from which he awoke from time to time, exhorting his followers to live like affectionate brothers.

Tradition says that just before the end, Buddha uttered a prophecy:

"A hundred years after I enter complete nirvana there will be a king in the town of Pataliputra, by the name of Asoka, who will rule over all four quarters of the earth, will distribute my reliquaries and establish eighty-four thousand samghas."

Buddha was still alive with the coming of the dawn. He faced the sun and said:

"Behold now, brethren, this is my exhortation to you. Decay is inherent in all things. Assiduously, you should rid yourself of your dread of the end."

These were Buddha's last words. The year of his death was 483 B.C.

At the time of Buddha's death, Buddhism—as it came to be known—was still a minor sect of Hinduism. It would become a major creed, spread all over the world, through the work of Asoka the Great.

8

THE ROYAL CONVERT

As he was meditating near the gate of his palace one day, King Asoka noticed a young boy wearing the yellow garb of the Buddhist monk. Impressed by the boy's serious air, the king invited him into his chambers for a talk. The young monk's name was Nighroda, and he was to play a significant role in Asoka's life. The king asked him about the Buddhists' creed.

"Buddhists," Nighroda answered, "are indifferent to death but serious about immortality." These were words to be pondered over. Why should a mere boy be concerned with death, the king wondered, and be thinking of immortality? He asked Nighroda to return to the

palace with older sages who could answer his many
questions.

After a short while the boy returned, accompanied by
thirty-two Buddhist monks. They were learned men who
could instruct the king about the lofty thoughts of the
Enlightened One. They told Asoka about the many
temptations sprouting from human nature and about the
base desires one had to fight. It was these desires, they
said, that caused the sufferings of man. They also instructed the king in how he could purge himself of these
cravings. They told him that all life carried the spark of
the divine. Yes, all life, even that of the insect. The
insect of today might become a prince in the next life.

The yellow-robed Buddhists told the king about the
bliss of meditation, and the close kinship among the
members of the sect. They instructed him about the
duties of the *upasaka*, the lay devotee; the *ajivika*, the
religious mendicant; and the bhikkhu, the member of
the samgha, the hermitage.

When this visit took place, after the Kalinga War,
Asoka's mind was still fresh with the impressions of
death and pestilence, grieving women and children,
proud warriors, and the wailing slaves.

After this visit Nighroda and the thirty-two monks
vanished from Asoka's life, but not from his mind. Tradition holds—and much of Asoka's life story is based on
tradition—that it was the boy and the monks that turned
his thoughts to the Buddhist creed.

According to another tradition, the saintly Upagupta,
the son of Gupta, was the one who converted Asoka to

the creed of Buddha. The ascetic dwelt on Mount Uru-munda, in the Natabathika forest near Natura, and there he was visited by the king. According to another version, the saint dwelt in Benares, the most sacred city in all India on the bank of the holy Ganges.

The king asked the sage to instruct him in the thoughts of the illustrious Buddha. After a while the saintly man turned up with eighteen thousand monks. Whether they all took turns in instructing the king or whether Upagupta alone imparted the instruction, the legend does not say.

Asoka had been a Brahmanic Hindu before his con-version, particularly devoted to Siva, whose name signi-fies "happy" in Sanskrit. Since Siva was an "all-purpose god," he was not always happy, a divinity with a complex personality to reconcile his functions as both creator and destroyer. He was the master of time, among many other things, also of justice, water, and the sun. Cor-responding to his thousand functions, he had a thousand names. To perform all his tasks he had five heads, three eyes, one located in the center of his forehead, and ten hands. Siva wore a garland of human skulls, serving as his symbol of the destroyer, and also a serpent necklace, the sign of eternity.

Hinduism was a complex religion, filled with gods like Siva. Buddhism, in comparison, must have impressed Asoka as refreshingly simple. After his change of heart in the wake of the Kalinga War, he was ready to hail a religion which sanctified life. The Enlightened One had said that there was a god—within oneself, one's own conscience. How much more helpful was such a god, in comparison with Siva? And how did one find that god? There was no need for intermediaries. Look for him in all sincerity and you will find him.

So Asoka became a Buddhist, although the exact time is not known. At that time Buddhists had no rituals, no hard and fast doctrines or dogmas. Becoming a Buddhist required no formal conversion. The so-called monks themselves were no priests. They were seekers after truth, purging their minds of earthly slag, and concentrating on meditation. Nor did the Buddhists consider themselves a different sect from the Hindus. There were several varieties of Hinduism, and the Buddhists formed one of these. It is for these reasons that we do not know when King Asoka embraced Buddhism. We do know, however, that this event occurred in the wake of the Kalinga War. The famous Kalinga Edict, carved into rock, spoke of the king's conversion: "That war [Kalinga] awakened in the king's breast feelings of remorse, profound sorrow and regret." And then the constant thought preying on the royal mind: "The loss of even the hundredth or thousandth part of the persons slain, taken captive and done to death at Kalinga, would now be a matter of profound regret to His Majesty."

Unique in the history of the human race are Asoka's thousands of memorial columns—it is assumed that there were that many of them—some of which are still in position to this day. They are the main evidence of the unique work of King Asoka. As a devotee completely committed to Buddhism and the missionary of the creed to which he pledged his soul, he undertook a pilgrimage twenty-four years after his ascension to the throne, in the footsteps of the Lord Buddha, accompanied by Upagupta, the sage.

Starting from Pataliputra, the king and the wise man proceeded northward on the royal road to Nepal. As they traveled farther away from the capital, they approached the foothills of the awe-inspiring Himalayan range. They veered westward, seeking the Lumbini garden, and they found the hallowed place of the miraculous birth. "Here, Great King," Upagupta addressed Asoka, "the Venerable One was born. Here, a minute after his birth, he took the seven steps. . . ."

On that spot Asoka had one of his pillars inscribed. Nature was unkind to this memento, and it became buried in the debris of countless centuries. Not only was it buried but it was also completely forgotten. More than twenty-one centuries later, in 1896, it was discovered and restored to its original location.

From the Lumbini garden the saintly Upagupta guided the steps of his royal disciple to Kapilavastu, the childhood home of Gautama. It had fallen into decay long before, and was now a marshy jungle, a sanctuary for birds and beasts.

The sage and the royal convert, continuing their pilgrimage, proceeded from there to the most hallowed place of their creed. This was the spot where Buddha had his illumination, in the deer park of Sarnath, four miles from the sacred city of Benares. In that park Gautama had launched his reforming movement and set forth the Eightfold Path.

There Asoka honored the Enlightened One in the royal manner. He ordered the carving of a monumental pillar—*lat*—seventy feet high. When the Chinese missionary pilgrim, Hiuen Tsang, saw it in the seventh century of the Christian era, it was still in its full splendor. "It shines and sparkles like a mirror," wrote the pilgrim. "Its smooth surface is like ice and the outlines of Buddha may be seen on it permanently."

This beautiful piece of craftsmanship on polished sandstone was probably the work of master artists whom Asoka had invited from Persia. They topped the lat by the likeness of four lions representing the master's four Noble Truths. Below them they placed the *dharmachakra*, the wheel of faith, representing the endless cycle of births and deaths, rebirths and deaths again, the life-giving force of the sun, the inevitable ups and downs of life.

The artists adorned the column with the likenesses of four animals: a bull, representing the west; an elephant the east; a horse the south; and a lion the north. They were to show that all parts of the globe were subject to dharma's eternal laws. Carved into the shaft was a portion of one of Asoka's famous sermons in stone: "Thus the Beloved of the Gods [Asoka] proclaims that religion must not be divided. . . ."

Hiuen Tsang found other historic mementos, too, in the deer park: a monastery for fifteen hundred monks;

a *stupa*, reliquary chamber; and a colossal image of Buddha the Enlightened One sitting on his lion throne. The rain, the wind, the soil, and man buried these evidences of the past. The British government, India's ruler at the time, brought them to life again, beginning in 1904, and the lat, a pride of Indian art, is one of the country's greatest treasures in the museum at Sarnath.

When India became independent in 1947, it had to decide upon official symbols. It selected the lion capital of the Asokan pillar, and his wheel, in spite of the fact that the overwhelming majority of the people of India were Hindus, not Buddhists. The immortality of Asoka thus became embedded in the origins and history of free India, which considered the missionary ruler its most famous son.

Always in the footsteps of Gautama, the royal pilgrim went on his way. His next stop was Sravasti, the capital of Kosala, one of the six great cities of India at the time of Buddha. There Devadatta, the incarnation of evil, attempted to kill Gautama, and was swallowed by the enraged earth.

The next station for the royal pilgrim and his guide was Bodha Gaya where the Buddha received the enlightenment which inaugurated a new age in his life and also that of Asian humanity. Upagupta told the king the strange legend of the creation of Gaya, and there were many amazing events in the land of India in those days. This was the story of a monster for whom the huge outcropping of granite near the shrine was named. Even today Hindus worship that stone. In those days the dwelling of Yama, lord of Hell, was nearby and that potentate was spoiling for a show of force so as to make the monster his slave. However, Gaya put up a terrible fight and would have won if it had not been for the last-minute intercession of Lord Visnu, who turned the creature into the rock that is still a place of pilgrimage.

At Kusinagara, King Asoka's year-long pilgrimage ended, at the very spot that the Enlightened One entered upon the first stage of his nirvana. There it was that Buddha uttered his prophecy.

On his trip the royal pilgrim performed many noble deeds. To worthy people he granted the remission of their taxes, and he distributed lavish gifts to people dwelling near the holy sites. He ordered reliquary chambers of Buddha built in many places—cylindrical mounds of stone, brick, and earth, often of majestic proportions. There is even a legend about how many there were.

This time, according to the legend, Asoka asked the opinion of a sainted man, Moggaliputra Tissa. The ruler asked his question in a roundabout way: "How many parts does the human body comprise?" And the sage replied without a second's hesitation: "Eighty-four thousand parts." So King Asoka gave orders for the building of eighty-four thousand monasteries and reliquaries, each to contain a portion of the Buddha's body.

An especially large number of these was built in the eastern plains of the Ganges, where Buddha carried on much of his work. The Sanskrit word for monastery is *vihara,* and that part of India is still called Bihar, one of the states of the republic today.

Legends come easy to the people of India, and there is another one to explain the vast number of shrines. According to this version, Asoka asked this question of the sage: "How many sections are there in the dharma [duties of the individual] as taught by the master?" And the wise man answered: "Eighty-four thousand sections."

To this the king replied: "Each of these sections I will honor with a vihara."

Hiuen Tsang claims to have seen a likeness of Asoka wearing the garment of a Buddhist monk in one of the monasteries. This was several centuries after the king's death. That likeness has vanished and no representation of Asoka has ever been found.

The works of art created during Asoka's reign to honor the Enlightened One were, according to Sir John Marshall, the British art critic, "masterpieces in point of both style and technique, the finest carvings, indeed, that India has yet produced and unsurpassed . . . by anything of their kind in the ancient world."

Another critic, Vincent A. Smith, said: "The skill of the stonecutter may be said to have attained perfection and to have accomplished tasks which would, perhaps, be found beyond the powers of the twentieth century. Gigantic shafts of hard stone, thirty or forty feet in length, were dressed and proportioned with the utmost nicety, receiving a polish which no modern mason knows how to impart to the material."

Works of this kind require not only great technical skill but also real artistry. The fact that the masses of the people admired such art indicates an unusually high level of culture. It must be kept in mind that these magnificent works were created twenty-two centuries ago.

9

✿ ROYAL SERMONS IN STONE

At the fork of the highway a large group of people had gathered. They sat on the ground or stood looking intently at the seventy-foot-high pillar.

Even though it was still early morning, the piercing sun began to numb the senses, so that many people sought shelter under the widespread crown of a banyan tree. There were all kinds of people in the crowd: noblemen in richly ornamented palanquins atop their towering elephants; tradesmen on their way to the marketplaces; artisans and peasants, too.

Buddhist monks attempted to explain the meaning of the shaft. It was a new message carved in stone, the words of King Asoka, beloved of the gods, of gracious mien.

Today we know of about thirty-five of these memorial columns. They are carved upon rocks, pillars, boulders, and cave walls. Shorter "documents" of this kind include dedications, brief commentaries, and related matters. Through these carvings we have acquired much of our knowledge about the king. From these stones we know about Asoka's deeds, his missionary work for Buddhism at home and abroad, about his teachings, and his policies, domestic and foreign. He speaks in the third person, and the name of Asoka never appears. He refers to himself as "beloved of the gods" and "of gracious mien." Most information about the king not carved into stone is legend.

These carvings were set up where the largest concourse of people could see them. Asoka addressed himself to the masses, as he was a missionary to his people and wanted to be heeded. Many of his edicts and pillars have been found in the most densely settled area, the Gangetic plains. Others were installed in prominent places near the foothills of the high mountains. Some of these "sermons in stone" were found as far north as Kashmir and as far south as Sidapura, as far east as Tosali, and as far west as the farthest Indus River tributaries.

The people of India, then as now, spoke "hundreds of tongues," and, therefore, common idioms for the sermons in stone had to be found. The language used was West Asokan, a variant of Prakrit, derived from the literary Sanskrit, the oldest language of the Indo-European family, of which English is one of the offsprings. The edicts used two types of scripts. One of these was written from right to left, the same as Hebrew and Arabic, and it may have originated in the eastern Mediterranean region, related to Aramaic, the language of Christ. The other script was written from left to right, in the way of the Indo-European languages. In 1837 an English official in India, James Prinsep, deciphered the script used on the Asokan rock and pillar edicts.

The texts add up to about five thousand words, and some of them have lent themselves to varying interpretations. Indeed, much of the "Asoka scholarship" deals with reading and interpreting the edicts. As the king himself said in one of his texts, by way of an apology, the space was often limited and some of his scribes made mistakes. Also the elements of nature, wind and rain, wrought havoc with the stones.

The very existence of the edicts justifies the conclusion that there must have been a sufficiently large number of people in the land to make this expensive means of communication worthwhile. There are large areas of the world even today where it would make no sense to have such edicts installed since few of the people can read.

"It is impossible for any student to read the edicts with care," commented Vincent A. Smith, a former official of Britain's Indian civil service, "and not hear the king himself. . . . We can discern a man of strong will, unwearied application, and high aims, who spared no labor in the pursuit of ideals, possessed the mental grasp capable of forcing the vast conception of missionary enterprise on three continents and was, at the same time, able to control the intricate affairs of church and state in an empire which the most powerful sovereign might envy."

The basis of all of Asoka's edicts was that people should conduct themselves in harmony with dharma, the laws of morality, and that there was no greater god than truth. Asoka assured his people that wherever he happened to be he was always concerned with their welfare, and that the people of his domains constituted a brotherhood. He recalled that the harm done to one hurt the entire community, since all the people formed units of common aspiration and were seekers of a common goal. He said that people who were shedding blood in aggressive wars were acting in contravention of morality. He stressed this particularly in his Kalinga Edict, the lofty principles of which were ahead of his time and of our age as well.

As for Buddhism, the immortal missionary saw it not as a new religion but as the reinterpretation of Hinduism. Asoka reasoned that the orthodox followers of the Hindu faith were bewildered rather than helped by the complications of their creed. Which of the forty crores of gods should they pamper, to which should they offer sacrifice? Which of these hundreds of millions of gods were useful to their followers? How great was the might of the gods that dwelt on the mountains peaks, in the dense woods, in the waters, on the overheated rocks? How could one pacify a god so petty that his wrath was aroused merely because a person worshiped a rival?

With Buddhism it was different. There were no gods wearing human or animal faces, and certainly Buddha was not one of these. He had not claimed to be even a religious reformer. But there was the supreme goal and value—truth—concealed in each person. No jealous gods, no greedy priests.

Asoka's sermons in stone are impressive today because they seem to be the work of a twentieth-century man. He was a pioneer in the type of statecraft in which the government attempted to unite the creative forces of the entire community for the peoples' mutual benefit.

In foreign affairs, too, Asoka was ahead of the twentieth century. He sought to solve the problems of his domains by peaceful means. After the Kalinga conflict, he became convinced that there were no victors in wars. What Asoka did not say in his edicts was also of great weight. He did not say, for instance, one harsh word against any foreign country, tribe, or clan.

Since the thoughts of Asoka were carved into stone —and his were important thoughts, especially in that age—we must review the more important samples of his work.

Fourteen Rock Edicts have been recovered, and they are the best records of Asoka's reign. Seven Pillar Edicts have been deciphered, throwing additional light on the thinking of the king. Special issues of his "autobiography in stone," such as the Kalinga Edict, tell about the

historic events that brought about the dramatic change
of heart from warrior to a man of peace.

In his stone autobiography Asoka calls himself the
"beloved of the gods." We know, of course, that there
are countless gods in Hindu-Brahmanism, but Asoka
had become a Buddhist. Why, then, did he speak of
gods? The Enlightened One did not claim that he was
godlike, although legend did claim mastery of the world
for his thoughts. Buddhism professed no belief in gods
with human features. There was only one god, it claimed,
and it was dharma—duty, truth, and virtue—a god without a human face.

Never once did Asoka himself invoke the aid of any
god, Hindu or otherwise, in his edicts. Never did he call
upon Visnu, Brahma, Krishna, or any of the others. Nor
did he invoke the name of Buddha. So, why did he call
himself the beloved of gods? Because he reigned over
people, most of whom were, we assume, Hindus, whom
he wanted to see in the ethical school of the Enlightened
One, but did not want to antagonize. He was doing his
missionary work with discretion and care.

A basic teaching of Asoka is contained in his First
Rock Edict, which declared that life was sacred. Not
only was the life of man sanctified, but all lives, including animals'. This was in harmony with Buddha's
teachings. Also, this was in line with the principle of
reincarnation. One may be a prince today and a ram
in the next life, or any other kind of animal. In this
edict Asoka went beyond announcing a religious principle. He was not preaching one thing and doing some-

thing else. There were no more samayas in his household, he said—the feast orgies at which animals were slaughtered.

We have the picture of a "welfare state" in Asoka's Second Rock Edict. Travel was important in the country for traders and also for the many nomads. Much of the time the land is excruciatingly hot, a "land in flames." Many lives must have been lost because there were no wells. In this stone record of his reign Asoka said: "Wells have been dug on the roads and trees planted for the travelers' benefit."

In this record we also have the first mention of "social medicine." Asoka's concern, it seems, was motivated by a tragic accident. Word had reached him about a gentle monk who died while traveling, because of the absence of suitable medicine. "Medicinal herbs, wholesome for man and beast," says the edict, "have been caused to be cultivated and brought into the land. . . . Roots and fruits have also been imported and planted everywhere."

We can almost see the pleased smile on the king's face when recalling the aid that his work brought to his people. Such concern was unusual in those days and is not really common even today.

Asoka's "Sermon on the Mount" has been the designation of the Third Rock Edict, one of the most substantial, dealing with several phases of the royal policy, proclaiming his humanitarian creed.

"Commendable is the service of the father and mother," the edict says, "and so is liberality to friends, neighbors, Brahmans and sramanas [ascetics]." Then the king mentions a virtue which is not widely held even today: "It is commendable not to hoard too much gold; to borrow little and to refrain from exploiting others."

In the same edict Asoka instructs his subordinates to be the servants of his people, not their masters. He tells them to undertake tours of inspection so as to familiarize themselves with the public needs. He further instructs them to become the peoples' teachers by disseminating the knowledge of dharma. Thus the kingdom of Magadha was to be dedicated to high ethical aims, becoming a consecrated community where moral law was to rule.

A confession of past failings is included in the Fourth Rock Edict. Avarice, hatred, and martial pageants had been his vices, the king admits. From these evils he turned to the virtues of charity, compassion, and religious pilgrimages. "The sound of the war-kettles has been transformed into the call to dharma. . . ." In the same edict, Asoka calls upon his offspring to follow in his footsteps so that people should learn from their lessons and deeds. In this "sermon" Asoka turns against hypocrisy, saying that piety should be practiced, not merely professed.

An important innovation in the reign of Asoka is dealt with in this "sermon"—the *dharmamatras*, or morality officers.

"In the past there were no [such] officers but I have appointed them since my coronation thirteen years ago. Together with the votaries of all faiths they should be engaged in laying the foundations of morality, promoting the weal of all who are dedicated to dharma in their present or later lives. . . . [The officers] are to work among the servants and masters, the Brahmans, the destitute and aged people—for the benefit of them all. They should aid also those who are in jail, shielding them against harassment, and securing release for those who have large families or are overwhelmed by calamities and heavily burdened by age. . . ."

"Benevolence is difficult," says the same edict, "and he who performs such acts accomplishes a difficult deed. I have performed much that is difficult. Reprehensible is he who neglects acts of benevolence, and it is easy, indeed, to sin."

This edict has been subject to many interpretations. There were caste barriers in Asoka's time, and by mentioning masters, servants, Brahmans, and destitutes in the same sentence he may have suggested "integration" and the weakening of the castes.

The dharmamatras were to perform a double function. They were to be lay preachers and executive organs of the government. In the latter capacity they were to receive the peoples' complaints against official harassment. In this respect, too, Asoka was centuries ahead of his time. It is only now that some advanced countries have established an office to protect the interests of the individual against governmental authority. It is known today as *ombudsman.*

In modern times Asoka has sometimes been criticized for the dharmamatras. The critics describe these officials as governmental busybodies and police agents. Obviously, one cannot judge the nature of the work of these officials from this distance, but it does not seem to have been in Asoka's mind to let them perform the functions of police spies.

"At all times," Asoka says in the Fifth Rock Edict, "in the women's quarters, or when I am eating, in my private chambers, in my mews, in my conveyance, on the pleasure grounds, everywhere the persons appointed to observe should keep me informed of the peoples' business . . . I never feel at ease unless I can exert myself to the full in the dispatch of public business. I must work for the peoples' welfare."

The Sixth Edict is a repetition of the previous one, while the Seventh deals with a basic problem, religious harmony in a land of diverse ways. "People are of different inclinations and passions . . ." says this edict, "and commendable is the restraint of passion, also inner purity, steadfastness, and gratitude." Then the ardent wish of Asoka: "The king desires that all sects may live [freely] everywhere in the land."

In the Eighth Rock Edict the king could not refrain from a little boasting. "Other rulers make it a practice," says this writ, "to sally forth on pleasure trips, the chase and other diversions. But I went on a pilgrimage to the site of the sambodhi [enlightenment of the Lord Buddha]. Thence I proceeded to supervise the work of the morality officers, also paying visits and giving gifts to Brahmans, ascetics, elders, and country folk, instructing and testing them in the precepts of piety. The pleasure of such visits surpasses everything else."

Obviously a follower of Buddha, the king did not withhold his gifts from the followers of other creeds—Brahmans, for instance, as attested by this carved sermon. Thus he demonstrated anew that he practiced the virtue of religious harmony and not merely preached it.

The Edict of the True Ceremonial is the designation of the Ninth Edict, in which Asoka takes a stand against the Brahmans' practice of representing ceremonies as the substance of religion. "Ceremonies should be performed if they promote morality." He meant, no doubt, that even though ceremonies induce moods, generating real religious sentiments, and thus may result in lofty deeds, they are sometimes mere shells of piety, without substance.

The edict contains an admonition to women, asking them to "stop frivolous business in your idle moments, gossiping, gambling, and flirting. Spend your time in the more profitable occupation of devising better protection for aliens and more human treatment for slaves." The same admonition, addressed to the entire community, is included in the Tenth Edict. Specifically, the ailing slave should be accorded more decent treatment.

If Asoka was concerned about slavery, why did he not abolish it? Why did he not see that slavery was not in harmony with dharma? Why did he not see any inconsistency between his lofty ideals and the unlofty practice of bondage? Because even though he was ahead of his time, he was a child of his age, which considered slavery an established institution, whose permanence was not questioned, just as it did not occur to the authors of the

American Declaration of Independence that there was
an inconsistency between slavery and their inspired
words: "We hold these truths to be self-evident, that all
men are created equal, that they are endowed by their
creator with certain unalienable rights. . . ."

"Morality is difficult to achieve for the lowly as well
as for the highly placed," Asoka says in the same edict.
"It is particularly so unless one attends to it with con-
centrated effort, renouncing [trivial] interests. It is much
harder for those of higher rank." It was obviously harder
because they could manipulate the sequence of events.
The founder of Christianity was to say a few centuries
later: "It is easier for the camel to go through the eye of
the needle than for the rich man to enter the kingdom
of God."

Like any other author of influence, a missionary,
apostle, a great teacher, Asoka often wondered if people
were heeding his words. It was in moments of such
doubt that he composed other edicts repeating earlier
points, as in the Eleventh and Twelfth Rock edicts:
"Observe dharma; be kind to your parents; be generous to
kith and kin; be decent to your slaves; morality is the
greatest gift."

In several of his stone sermons Asoka repeated: "You
are true to your own beliefs if you accord kindly treatment to adherents of other faiths. You harm your own
religion by harassing followers of other creeds." He also
implied that while decency to others was its own reward
it was also good for the future, by creating a stockpile of
merits to be used in another life.

The Kalinga War kept preying on Asoka's mind, and he refers to it in the Thirteenth Rock Edict: "Directly after the annexation of Kalinga, the king was stricken with remorse, since this victory entailed the peoples' maiming, killing and enslavement. . . . This was a matter of deep sorrow and regret to the king. . . . A country's conquest leads to the crushing of people whose ways may be different from our own, and this, too, was a matter of deep regret. . . . Therefore, the king resolved to exchange good for evil and to forsake violence. Therefore he bids his own people to turn from evil ways, since the king wishes to establish the reign of justice, security, peace, and mercy for all. Conquering hatred is the greatest victory, the king believes. And the greatest glory is the type of conquest that produces happiness. . . . The king has ordered these tablets to be prepared for this reason, having inscribed upon them the laws of piety, mercy and peace. That is the road to happiness in this life and the next."

The king appears in a double role in his appealing Fourteenth Rock Edict, in which he summarizes his previous points: "I have commanded these religious edicts on morality to be inscribed. Some of them are brief, others middling, while still others are long. Vast is the country; much has been written and more is to come. Because of the importance of some of these thoughts, they have been repeated over and over again, for the people to heed. Some parts are incomplete because of lack of space, damage to the stones or errors of the scribes."

Asoka wanted to make his mark, and he was burning with the desire to teach the people, to make a lasting impression on them, and to give them guidance in their lives. But he was assailed by doubts. Did he make his meaning clear? He asked his courtiers and they answered, no doubt: "They are masterpieces, Your Majesty."

We may only guess the sincere opinion of Asoka's subjects on his work, but we know what people today, centuries later, think about it. The work of Asoka has no parallel in history. At a crucial point of his life he had a change of heart and mind. He turned his back on the past when he had been unconcerned about the loss of human life. He found that life was a unique gift, the reproduction of the original creative force, and that to squander it was contrary to eternal laws. He learned, too, that the forces of life had their own rules, and that their name was "truth." Nature was true, and life was true, too.

From his master, the Lord Buddha, Asoka had learned how to find the truth, enfolded in the four noble truths, to which the Enlightened One had pointed, accessible to man with the aid of the eightfold path and the twenty-five virtues. The missionary king had set up a corps of teachers, his morality officers, to inculcate the values of truth in his people. His was a land which he hoped would not only profess, but would also live, according to the precepts of Buddha. It was in some of his pillar edicts that Asoka appeared most conspicuously in his favorite role as missionary teacher.

10

✤ THE PILLAR EDICTS

Sultan Feroz Shah, the fourteenth-century northern
Indian ruler, noticed on his travels two gigantic shafts
of hard sandstone, partly buried under subtropical vegetation. A closer view disclosed that their enormous surfaces were like mirrors. The royal traveler found one of
these in the northwest of India at a place called Topra,
near the town of Umballa. The other was found farther
east, at Meerut, in the United Provinces of India. Both
of these gigantic structures were located near the Hima-
laya foothills. These were two of Asoka's Pillar Edicts.

These pillars were genuine works of art, distributed
over an area including Allahabad, Benares, Meerut, and

the Nepal foothills—all sacred sites. They had round
polished monolithic shafts and elaborate capitals, consisting of a lotus bell, an abacus decorated with geese,
palmettos, and Buddhist symbols, with a crowning sculpture in the round consisting of one or more animals.
Their average height was forty to fifty feet, but some of
them, such as those sighted by Feroz Shah, were higher.

These works of arts, created under the reign of Asoka,
owe much to western influence, and, indeed, it has been
argued that they have been created by western crafts-
men. It seems certain that Asoka was in contact with
the artists of the Seleucid houses, descendants of Alexander the Great.

Feroz decided to have the shafts transported to Delhi,
his capital city. To issue the order was easy; to carry it out
was not.

First, the shafts had to be wrapped in the shavings of
soft silk-cotton trees. Then cushioned temporary "beds"
had to be prepared on the ground. A swarm of workers
dug deep into the soil to detach the monumental bases
upon which the towering shafts stood. The shafts were,
in turn, lowered to the ground and placed upon the
earthen beds.

The next problem was transportation. Some of the
roads were less than sketchy, and little more than trails.
Since no existing carriage was large enough for the shafts,
new vehicles of tremendous size had to be fashioned.
Each had forty-two wheels, instead of the customary
four. To prevent harm to the surface of the shafts, they

were encased in layers of animal skins and reed. Thousands of slaves were employed to heave the pillars from their earthen beds onto the gigantic conveyances. All was now set for the risky trip.

Since horses were unable to handle the loads, manpower had to be used. Stout ropes were attached to the vehicles and each huge segment was pulled by two hundred men. Altogether, some 8,400 people were needed for the operation. For days the vehicles inched their way across swamps and woods, hills and streams, on the primitive trails. The fate of Asoka's shafts was of the utmost importance to the Shah. He was not so concerned about the fate of men, and many slaves perished along the way. In the end, the pillars reached their destination on the outskirts of Delhi without as much as a scratch. There they were to proclaim the glory of King Asoka's reign and the glorious history of India.

The pillar sermons had one theme of paramount importance. Two words express that theme: *Satyameva Jayate*—nothing surpasses truth. Indeed, truth is God.

The Seventh Pillar Edict contains a summary of the royal missionary's main line of thought. Translated into modern language, it says that the responsibility for our deeds is ours, and should not be shifted to the gods. We are godlike, if we want to be, since god is in all of us. Every person therefore should act as if he were a saint, a future Buddha, a member of the consecrated community, the name of which is mankind. There is no sense in burning incense or offering any other kind of sacrifice to the gods. If a god can be bribed this way, then he is not a real god.

Asoka penetrated deep into the hearts of men, and what he found can be read on the burnished surfaces of his pillars: "A person sees only his own good deeds and boasts: 'I am the author of this deed.' In no wise does a person see his ill-deeds and confesses: 'I am the author of this ill-deed, or this act of impiety.'"

Then came the refrain, which Asoka had been repeating over and over again: "There is an eternal law, which keeps the world moving. The name of this is the law of piety."

"The need is for the application of the law of piety," the Pillar Edict says, "—intense self-examination, obedience, dread (of impious acts), and intense effort."

Asoka was an optimist. He believed that his words were heeded, and so he wrote: "Owing to my teaching, this desire for the law of piety, and the obligation of constantly observing the law, have grown and will continue growing."

The practical application of Asoka's teaching was *ahimsa*—forsaking violence, war, and bloodshed. Violence begets more violence, wars are the breeding grounds of more wars. If wars appear to solve some problems, the solutions are only for a limited time. New complications arise in the place of the presumed solutions. The vicious circle performs its endless rounds.

Was Asoka's teaching really effective? India's history provides only the partial answer. Many centuries after his reign India produced a man whom his contemporaries called the "Great Soul." This man was Gandhi, and he enjoined upon the people of India that ahimsa was the only solution, and that the name of his supreme God was truth.

11

✻ LIFE UNDER ASOKA

Asoka's palace was still standing when the Chinese pilgrim, Fa-Hsien, visited Pataliputra at the beginning of the fifth century of the Christian era. Fa-Hsien thought the palace so magnificent that he attributed its erection to supernatural forces. "The royal palace and halls in the midst of the city," he wrote, "which exist now as of old, were all constructed by the spirits that he [Asoka] employed. They piled up the stones, erected the walls and gates, executed the elegant carvings and inlaid sculpture work in a way no human hands in this world could do."

These alleged builders of Asoka's palace could not prevent its decay. The stately edifices have vanished, most of their remains buried in the ground, below the silt of the Ganges and Son rivers, under the city of Patna. "Slight and desultory excavations," says V. A. Smith, "have revealed enough to attest the substantial truth of the pilgrim's enthusiastic description and I have seen two huge and finely carved sandstone capitals—one with the acanthus-leaf ornament—dug up near Bankipur."

The numerous and magnificent monasteries founded by Asoka have shared the fate of his palaces. The only buildings of his period which remain in a state of tolerable preservation are those forming the celebrated group of *stupas* at and near Sanchi, in Central India, not very far from Ujjain, where Asoka held court as viceroy of the west before his accession to the throne.

The history and climate of India explain the condition of these historic remains. Few regions have been devastated by as many waves of invaders as this peninsula, the victim of countless generations of conquerors. The climate of the part of India where Asoka spent most of his life has done the rest of the damage—the torrential monsoon rains, the savage heat, and the wild vegetation which takes over every inch of space as soon as it becomes untenanted.

Still, it is possible to reconstruct life in those days. What was the day of Asoka like? How did he appear to his people? Did he actually practice what he preached? From fragments of contemporary accounts some of the details of his daily life may be reconstructed.

In that part of India, most of a man's work had to be performed before and after the sun stood high in the sky and had wilted all energy. Asoka rose from his couch at early dawn to the mellow sound of lutes. He proceeded to his private chambers where his subordinates had prepared his daily program. Waiting for the royal audience were his *rajukas*, viceroys, some of them from distant lands. He gave them instructions, and asked them for their reports. He heard complaints about the stewardship of some of them. Asoka was not only their supreme master but also the missionary preacher, and he reminded them of the moral law.

Also waiting for the monarch in the audience chamber were the dharmamatras, and their work was important for the realm. They were to disseminate the teachings of dharma. Through them the king kept in touch with his people, and through them, too, the laws of piety—and more especially of ahimsa, no violence—were upheld.

King Asoka selected for this task only those whom he could trust. But he knew that even the most trusted public officials had to be supervised. He recalled the popular saying: "Just as it is impossible not to taste honey on the tip of one's tongue, so it is impossible for government agents not to get a cut of the royal income." Therefore, the king had other officers to keep their eyes on the ethics of his morality officers.

After these interviews, the king retired to his inner chambers, to become spiritually and physically refreshed for the rest of the day. He took his bath, was massaged, and sat down to his first meal of the day. Then he refreshed himself spiritually by reading some of the sayings of Lord Buddha. Thus prepared, he proceeded again to his working chambers. Court trumpeters announced his approach to the audience hall. Asoka knew that people liked their king to live like a king.

In the audience hall the king came face to face with the realities of life. The hall contained a throng of petitioners, and others appealing to him in their litigations.

The reaction of the people to his august presence varied. Some of them were so awed that they fainted away at his feet. Others overreached themselves in fawning upon him. They assured him that his fame was greater than that of Lord Krishna the Great, and that his royal countenance was more radiant than the midday sun. To prove that, they shaded their eyes. We may assume that the king was not impressed by such flattery.

Still others among the petitioners approached the king as the supreme justice of final appeal. As the fountainhead of the law of the land and the source of mercy, he gave the word that bound and freed. Was he always just? Probably not, since he was human. But we may assume that he tried to be.

During the searingly hot season, the spring and summer, much of the work was crowded into the early morning hours. When the sun approached its zenith and the heat became oppressive, the audiences were over. Yet, this was not quite the end of the king's work.

He had his scouts search the country for learned men to instruct him in the incidents and thoughts of the Lord Buddha and to help him with their advice. It was his custom to confer with these men after his morning chores. Only then did he have his midday meal, after which he had another cooling bath. By that time the air was sultry and Asoka spent the time in his inner chambers with more study.

After the heat had somewhat abated, Asoka proceeded into the garden of his palace. He had a small zoo there of young animals such as playful tiger cubs, a baby elephant, and a bison. He liked to watch the pompous peacocks, the greedy parrots, and the domesticated pheasants. Wandering about the palace grounds he inhaled the fragrance of the exotic flowers and of the blooms of the trees.

In the twilight hours the king again attended to the affairs of the state, receiving the reports of palace officials and tax collectors, planning policies, organizing official trips, meditating on the text of new sermons in stone.

Asoka was not content with getting secondhand reports about the state of affairs in his country. He wanted to see what was going on, how his officials were doing, and how the people reacted to his teachings. Governing Magadha was a hard task. The people occupied all levels of civilization, from the lowest in obscure places of dense jungles, to the highest—the community of highly learned men. The people pursued numerous occupations, spoke many tongues, belonged to diverse castes and creeds. The India of Asoka was not merely a country —it was a world and, it seemed to many people, a world without end.

The king had other tasks, too. Asoka occupies a unique place in the history of the world because he was a man of peace. It was his policy to wage no aggressive war. But not all the people of the world outside of India were men of peace. Therefore, Asoka could not afford to let his guard down. He had to have armed forces for defense, and keeping them in trim required work.

The infantry was the core of his army, and it consisted of three separate contingents: professional warriors, tribal levies, and the foot soldiers paid by urban merchants. The professionals received compensation for their services. It was in exchange for their livelihood that the tribal soldiers served Asoka, since life in their native areas was particularly hard. The merchants had a special interest to keep the foe at bay, since in case of a lost war they were the ones to suffer most.

The most mobile force of Asoka's army was the war chariot. Such a vehicle was large, nine feet long and seven and a half feet wide, served by specially trained attendants. The chariots performed several functions: piercing the enemy lines, helping to seize strongholds, and repelling attacks. Also, they served as battering rams. In case of a rout of the regular forces, they served as rallying points. To scare the foe the charioteers uttered piercing battle cries—an early instance of psychological warfare.

Asoka's armed forces also contained battle elephants. The huge beasts served as "movable fortifications" and living "heavy tanks." They could cross difficult terrain which would have wrecked the chariots. The animals formed uninterrupted lines of protective walls when needed. They had one serious drawback, however. If they did panic, there was no telling what they might do.

Asoka also had a cavalry and a small navy, both of which he used more for the propagation of peace than defense. The cavalry was called upon to carry missionaries overland, across the passes of the world's highest mountains, while the navy helped to convey Asoka's Buddhist message to the islands of the South China Sea.

A government performing so many functions was expensive to run. Therefore, the treasury had to be well-provided. Taxes were high and they contained some unusual features—unusual even for man in the age of high taxation.

Since farming was the principal occupation of the people, taxes on land formed the main revenue sources. Asoka himself was the most important landlord, and received a large income from that source. He had his fields tilled by people who today would be called sharecroppers, and they received half of what they produced. The arrangement was not bad for his workers. Even today sharecroppers in the underdeveloped part of the world sometimes get no more than one-fifth of what they produce.

The bulk of the arable land was in private hands, and the governmental tax collector received a quarter of the revenue. That is about what the average American citizen has to hand to the tax collector today.

Taxes on trade were higher, since commerce was more profitable than farming. Then, too, merchants were more costly to the king. They had to have special protection from the bandits, who were likely to lurk in the dense jungles along the travel arteries. Besides, the traders benefited from the special conveniences provided by the king, as, for instance, the roadhouses, the shady trees along the public roads, and the community wells.

We have a fairly good picture of urban life in the records of the Greek historian-diplomat Megasthenes, and also in those of a contemporary of Asoka.

Urban life was important. The most important towns were trading and governmental centers in key positions along the natural highways, which were the streams. Benares, one of the most ancient cities of the world, was already in existence then, under the name of Kashi. Other famous cities were Prayag—today called Allahabad —Mathura, and Indrapashtra. The foothills of the mountain ranges contained many towns, as, for instance, Rampurwa, the site of one of Asoka's pillar edicts, Lauriya, Ruminidi, and Sravasti. Important places in the west were Taxila and Peshawar, and Maski in the extreme south. But the most important city was, of course, the capital, Pataliputra.

A visit to the capital during Asoka's reign was an exercise in wonderment. Extending for miles along the Ganges, the capital was awesomely impressive. As a shield against attacking foes and rampaging floods, the city was protected by tall walls, one side of which was the *bund*, an artificial embankment. The wall was forty feet high in parts, especially massive near the base, and tapering upward, provided with projecting rectangular outworks. Within this fortification there was another one, manned by crack archers of the realm.

Following an ancient model in urban planning, the streets were laid out in parallel patterns, each of them some thirty feet wide. The sections of the capital were divided into oblong blocks, for administrative and defense reasons. Entrances to the houses were mainly by way of side lanes rather than through the thoroughfares, providing a greater measure of privacy. Chutes on the outside walls of the better homes discharged waste matter into jars, removed by low-caste servants.

Wealthy people furnished their homes with heavy furniture of teakwood, inlaid with shells of green and blue. The houses of the rich townsmen were divided into quarters for men and women, and they were surrounded by gardens planted with flowers and fruit trees. Occasionally, the gardens contained ornamental ponds. If the owner was particularly affluent, his house contained a terrace on which he held social get-togethers on moonlit nights.

The day in the life of a rich man in Asoka's domains would begin with the daily bath, after which he was rubbed down with perfumed ointments, while his lips were reddened with dye. Then he put on his clothes consisting of a lower garment of fine linen or silk, often colored, and high-quality upper clothing, which betokened not only wealth but also good breeding.

The rich man's food was varied, but even he consumed no more than two meals a day. His main staples were barley, rice, and milk. Meat was served in wealthy houses, even though it entailed the slaughtering of animals, frowned upon by the king. The people of Magadha fancied many drinks, some of them exotic, as, for instance, the one distilled out of molasses and the honey-filled blossoms of the mahua tree. Another drink was fermented from finely powdered rice. Wine was popular, too, both sweet and dry. Drinking seems to have been a vice of the age which Asoka wanted to discourage, and so he appointed some of his morality officers as "sniffling sleuths," to track down the telltale scent of drinks. Eventually he had to compromise, however. He authorized stores to sell only small quantities of intoxicating drinks to "persons of good character."

The Indian peninsula was famed for its wealth in jewels, and in centuries to come it was the goal of countless adventurers bent on filling their bags with priceless gems. The rich people in Asoka's days liked to display their wealth and adorn their bodies by flaunting their collection of precious stones—agate, aquamarine, beryl, cat's-eye, jasper, topaz, and many more. These gems were worked into ornamental jewelry, as, for instance, intricately designed cross necklaces, with strands of beads crossed in the center, the ends attached to decorative girdles or hanging loose on both sides. The point of crossing of the jewelry was often covered by floral designs. Ornamental bangles and armlets were also enriched by precious stones. Rings were in great demand, usually four per person or at least two, and sometimes they were worn also on the thumbs. Even women whose husbands could not afford the high price of precious stones wore bangles, but they were copper or zinc.

A culture of an age is as good as its system of education. How good was education in Asoka's time?

Education was good, although, as can be expected, it was different from our educational ways. The school system had two dimensions, because of the interweaving of the spiritual with the practical, the sectarian and secular. Schools were imbued with the spirit of the Enlightened One. Boys who wanted to become monks had to serve in monasteries for ten years. It was recognized then, too, that education was as good as the educator. Because of that, promising students left the paternal house to live with their teachers. Even on the elementary level the curriculum was rich, including grammar, rhetoric, public policy, economics, and training in vocational arts and crafts. The student was preparing himself not only for this life but also for an endless sequence of lives after his presumed death—after his reincarnations.

Schools of higher learning—what we call colleges and universities—were scattered in the more populous parts of the kingdom of Magadha, in places such as Kashi (Benares), Ujjain, and Taxila. The best school seems to have been in Taxila, and its curriculum was rich. The scriptures formed the foundation of all higher learning, enriched by "the eighteen arts," a broad spectrum of studies including science fields, polity (government), linguistics, the use of the bow and the sword, horsemanship, elephant lore, and other disciplines, such as music and dancing. Because of the heat of the daylight hours, classes met from early dawn till noon.

For gifted or destitute students, scholarships were available. The gifted ones were instructed by "name" specialists. They were encouraged to engage in public discussions, so as to gain self-confidence in public speaking. Proving that Asoka's was truly an unusual age, teachers were adequately paid, and they could earn additional income by winning prizes in *parishads*, learned assemblies. The prizes were offered by the king.

Besides education, one can judge the quality of a culture by the level of public health. It must have been good, judging by references to it in Asoka's edicts. India was rich in medicinal herbs, and it also imported drugs and balms from faraway lands.

Because life—all life—was regarded as sacred, the health of the animals was also considered the concern of the state. It is said that an animal hospital in existence even in the late eighteenth century could be traced either to Asoka or to his influence. It was situated in the city of Surat, north of India's great western gateway, Bombay. An eyewitness described the hospital at length. It was called the Banyan Hospital, perhaps because of a stately banyan tree on its grounds. Enclosed by high walls so as to discourage the animal patients from leaving, it was divided into courts and wards. When an animal broke a leg or was otherwise disabled, his master took it to the hospital where it was received without regard to the caste or nationality of the owner. The wards contained not only horses, mules, cows, sheep, poultry, goats, monkeys, and a large collection of birds, but also an aged tortoise which was said to have been under hospital care for seventy-five years. Animals found a peaceful asylum also for the infirmities of age.

The most extraordinary ward was reserved for rats, mice, bugs, and many other kinds of noxious vermin. Suitable food was provided for all of them. All life was considered precious and immortal, and therefore this unusual collection of creatures.

We may assume that the average expectation of human life in India, as elsewhere, was short. The rich vegetation of the land, the combination of heat and moisture, provided not only food for people and beasts but supported legions of the vermin that shortened man's life: mosquitoes that infected the people with malaria; rats and other animals that carried the bubonic plague and other forms of pestilence.

Besides, the soil of India has a built-in tragedy. It is fantastically productive in many places, especially in the river valleys, when sun and rain are properly combined, and the monsoon rain is supposed to be a regular feature of India. But it is highly irregular, and if it is inadequate or spasmodic the productive soil turns disastrously unproductive. In that case the sun, normally a blessing, becomes a curse, and the soil a mass grave. The good earth, having turned vicious, becomes as hard as cement, and it produces nothing. Then the people die. That happens today, too, and it must have been a frequent occurrence in Asoka's days.

Besides education and sanitation, we measure the level of civilization by its penal laws. Where the laws are inhuman and cruel, the cultural level is low. Asoka held human—and every other—life in high esteem. Yet, in the application of stringent laws, he was not consistent. Some of his laws were overly strict.

Still, they were not as strict as the laws of some of the Western world as late as the beginning of the last century. Britain, for instance, imposed the death penalty then for what today are considered minor misdemeanors.

In spite of his high respect for life, Asoka did not abolish capital punishment. Death was the penalty for a number of deeds, including murder and depriving an artisan of the use of a hand or eye. We can draw the conclusion that the work of artisans was highly valued, perhaps because there was a shortage of them. Many of them must have been working for the king, carving his sermons on the pillars and stones. Death was also the penalty of tax-evaders. From this we can draw the conclusion that trying to evade taxes is not only a feature of the modern age. The person condemned to death was accorded a grace period of three days.

Asoka's laws provided for the loss of an eye for an eye, a tooth for a tooth, a customary procedure in early civilizations. Mutilation was the penalty for perjury and theft.

Most of the people in Asoka's time lived in villages, mainly on the Hindustan plain and along the streams. Although the peninsula has large cities today, most of the people still live in villages, of which there are more than five hundred thousand.

The difference in the way of life between the towns and hamlets was great, as it still is. Most of the people lived in mud huts covered with straw. The huts had no windows. In mountainous areas the dwellings were constructed of stone, and they occupied the outcroppings of rocks, wherever feasible, so as not to encroach upon fertile soil. The size of the hamlets depended upon the nature of the terrain, accessibility of water, and the quality of land. The peasant had to be near his field, and, therefore, the hamlets were scattered all over the land. Often the villages had to lead self-contained lives, separated by jungles, arid areas, and swamps. That is how India came to have so many languages and dialects—the number today is near seven hundred. A village of five-hundred families was considered large enough to be self-contained.

Common grazing grounds enabled the farmers to make better use of arable land. The household animals were usually driven home from the grazing ground at the approach of the twilight hours, so as to protect them against predatory beasts and men.

The villages had a measure of home rule, necessary because of their isolation. Such governments have been in existence since very ancient times and are still flourishing in the Republic of India today. Because they are composed of five people, usually elders, they are called *panchayats*, meaning five. The members of these local governing bodies were usually the heads of the better-to-do families. It was up to the panchayat to regulate communal matters of general interest, such as public works and minor infractions of the law.

Today India has countless castes in four vast groups,

and also outcastes, now called *harijans*—children of god—
to compensate them for their bitter lives. This designation was conferred upon them by the country's great
spiritual leader, the late Mahatma Gandhi. There were
castes in Asoka's day too, but not as numerous as today.
At that time they may have performed their original
function, as protective associations of vocational groups
against the exactions of the more influential people.

Trade was important to India. Some areas had surplus
produce in one commodity and a deficiency in others. An
exchange of goods had to take place. The sellers and
buyers met in traditional markets. In spite of the morality officers, public security was not always assured, as it
could not be in a country with jungles, swamps, deserts,
mountains, and rugged high plateaus. Because of these
difficulties, people proceeded to markets in caravans.
They loaded their salable produce on *sakatas*—bullock
carts—and armed themselves with bows and arrows.

If all went well, the travelers blessed Asoka for having
lined the lanes with trees in arid lands, so that they could
be refreshed in cooling shade. They also blessed his name
for the wells he provided.

The caravans eventually reached the marketplace,
where buyers and sellers met. Now the exciting business
of haggling began. Although royal ordinances set official
prices on main staples, people cared little about the listed
price. Haggling was an exciting game. The seller extolled
his merchandise which, he told the world, was fit only
for kings. The price he demanded was also suitable only
for royal pockets. In reply, the prospective buyer reviled

the offered goods, which he claimed were fit only for rats. While the sun proceeded on its climb to the top of the sky, the haggling continued, and eventually, the transaction was completed.

Because the traders' bags on the return trip were filled with *karshapana*—copper coins—it was more adventurous and, possibly, perilous. The copper coins were nicked with the buyers' distinguishing marks, but the bandits did not seem to care.

Most of the caravans must have returned to their hamlets safe and sound. Life was hard in India, and, therefore, who can blame the returning tradesman for wanting to have a good time. The best occasion for a celebration was a safe arrival. The king would have liked the traders to spend their time in meditation, but they preferred to participate in festivities. Itinerant actors performed scenes from India's glorious past, incidents taken from the sacred books. The relaxed traders relished the acrobats' stunning feats, the trained animals' antics, and the races of the fleet horses and the lumbering elephants.

Because of his puritanic streak, Asoka frowned upon games of chance. But he was practical-minded enough to know that he could not change human nature. Still he wanted to profit by it, and so he taxed the gambling dens in which the countrymen played *vibhitaka*, their favorite game of dice.

That is how the people lived in Asoka's day. They were living under the protection of the king, and the school system and sanitation were as good—if not better—than any in those days, not only in India but also in East and West. Asoka enjoined upon the people to turn to spiritual values, and be concerned with their place in the world and in future worlds. He was a human and humane ruler. He did everything in his power to keep in touch with his people, through his messages in stone, which manifested his concern. Some people consider his a "Golden Age." Perhaps it was, as much as any age can be, golden. It was certainly an unusual age, and Asoka was an unusual king. That is why the world honors him with the title of Asoka the Great.

12

✿ TO DISTANT LANDS

Asoka passed through various stages as he moved
closer to his master, Lord Buddha. In the year of the
Kalinga War, the ninth of his reign, he joined the Buddhist community as a layman. Two years later he became
a member of the order. In another two years, he set out
for sambodhi—Great Wisdom—entering upon the eightfold path in search of nirvana, the complete union with
nature, the end of all suffering, the absolute end, the
terminal point.

Even though the king was a dedicated Buddhist, the
hold of Hinduism continued. Priests—traditional Brah-

mans—now appeared increasingly in the guise of Buddhist monks, and Asoka became worried. He feared that
these so-called monks wanted to "reinterpret" Buddha
in line with their own interests.

The teachings of the Enlightened One appealed to
Asoka. They explained life simply, and his logical mind
liked that. In Hinduism, too many gods were fighting
one another, and they bit deeply into the subsistence of
the country, increasing their demands for sacrifices
through their priests. As the missionary of Buddha,
Asoka was also the high priest, the prophet. "Evil men
in yellow robes," he said, "have delivered false opinions
about the teachings of the Enlightened One." The false
opinions had to be removed so that Asoka could become
Buddhism's authentic missionary. How was this to be
done?

In preparation for extending his missionary activities,
Asoka wanted to hear from the sages the authentic
Word of Buddha. With that in mind, in 246 B.C. he
issued writs to a thousand sages to discuss and state
authoritatively the teachings of the Enlightened One.
The council met in Pataliputra.

Working closely with the sages, Asoka set forth the
basic principles of Buddhism, the official version, as
follows: carnal craving was the source of human pain;
pain could be eliminated by heeding the four noble
truths and by following the Eightfold Path toward
nirvana, the blissful absence of ignoble desires. God was
truth, the knowledge of which was imbedded in each
person, to be found by himself, with the aid of Buddha's

thoughts. Brahmans were not needed for the search.

After this historic council, Asoka ordered that "yellow-robed charlatans" should no longer pollute the sources of clear understanding. The removal of the charlatans was placed in the hands of the new government body— "Administration for the Preservation of Morals." Asoka also ordered that Buddha's teachings be collected in the Sanskrit language in a *pitaka*—"basket." Also, the king undertook the great task of dispatching missionaries to spread the Word of the Lord Buddha in all parts of the world. "They shall mix with the Brahmans and beggars," the king told the missionaries, "with the dread and the despised, both within the kingdom and in foreign lands." This was a clear indication that he wanted them to work among the common people, too.

Although Asoka himself was a Buddhist, he never persecuted Brahmanism. The two systems coexisted during his reign, and for a thousand years thereafter.

Buddhism had originated in the border areas of India. It had grown out of Brahmanism but developed features completely contrary to it. Yet Buddha never considered himself the leader of a reformation movement, and he did not quarrel with the Brahmans. It was not in his nature to quarrel with anyone. He had some followers in India, when Asoka came to spread his creed. The king, too, carried on no feud with the followers of the traditional faith. As a result of Asoka's work, Buddhism spread across the mountain ranges, into Tibet, China, and Mongolia. It spread into Japan and regions of Southeast Asia. From a small sect it developed into one of the world's leading religions, with tens of millions of followers.

Ceylon seems to have been the first country converted to Buddhism. The Greeks had known the island as *Taprobane*—"dusky leaves"—because of its lush vegetation. Many centuries later the Portuguese explorers renamed it Zelan. It became Buddhist as a result of Asoka's missionary efforts, and it has remained Buddhist to this day.

Miraculous, indeed, is the history of the conversion of Ceylon—miraculous, according to the legend. Asoka dispatched two of his children to King Tissa, the ruler of the island. Mahendra, twenty, wearing the monk's yellow robe, and his sister Sanghamitra, eighteen, were the royal missionaries.

Mahendra, who arrived in Ceylon before his sister, was so persuasive that Tissa's daughter, Princess Anula, and her five hundred attendants also wanted to enter the order. But there was a problem. Monks lacked the authority to ordain females. King Tissa, who wanted to please the princess, sent his nephew to Pataliputra with the request to send Sanghamitra to the island. To reinforce her effectiveness, she was to bring along a branch of Buddha's sacred bo tree. Ecstatic about the success of the mission, Asoka proceeded to the sacred grove, severed the branch of tree, and handed it to his daughter. The princess boarded the boat that was to take her to Ceylon.

According to Ceylonese legend, as the royal boat dashed across the water and the Great Ocean, the waves around it were stilled in the circumference of a league, "while flowers of many hues were blossoming around it and sweet melodies of music were filling the air." The princess reached her destination and ordained the maidens, while the ruler of Ceylon deposited the branch of the sacred tree in Mahamegha garden, which he dedicated to Lord Buddha.

The royal missionaries stayed on the island, devoting their lives to their apostolic work, and organizing a brotherhood. Finally, in the fifty-eighth year of his ordination, Prince Mahendra died on Ceylon, and was laid to rest in a large reliquary chamber. A year later his sister died, and was also buried on the island.

Remarkable developments were common, indeed, on the island of dusky leaves. It has a seven-thousand-foot mountain, the top of which is called Adam's Peak. A large hollow on it resembles the imprint of a gigantic human foot. Buddhists call it the footprint of Buddha, Hindus call it the footprint of Siva, and Muslims call it the footprint of Adam.

Buddhists have another, more famous, place of pilgrimage in Ceylon. This is the Dalada Maligawa, the most famous Buddhist edifice in the world. The temple enshrines the Tooth of Buddha, which legend says, had been taken there by Princess Sanghamitra, who had hidden it in her hair.

Religious and lay functions were not separated in Asoka's kingdom, and often the missionaries were his ambassadors, spreading the faith overland and overseas. The early Buddhist missionaries made journeys in all directions. Some of them traveled from India to China via two main routes. One was particularly difficult, across the tallest mountains of the world in northwest India, then the Taklamakan Desert in Central Asia, to North China. The other route was by sea across the Indian Ocean to South China ports.

Missionaries were dispatched to Southeast Asia, too, to Burma, Siam (Thailand today), Cambodia, Java, Borneo, and Malaya. For many centuries this area surrounding the South China Sea was a kind of "Farther India," ruled by Indian princes, filled with Indian traders, and instructed by Indian religions, mostly Buddhist.

Asoka also dispatched missionaries to the West. He sent ambassador-missionaries to King Alexander of Epirus, which is part of Greece today; to Antiochus Theos of Syria in the Levant, facing the easternmost Mediterranean; and to Ptolemy Philadelphos of Egypt. In most parts of the East, Buddhism took firm roots, but that is not true of the West.

Korea was the next stop on the victorious eastward march of Buddhism. Chinese monks performed most of the work of conversion. The rulers of the country were converted in the middle of the fifth century of the Christian era.

South Korea became the staging area of Buddhism into Japan. In the middle of the sixth century, the king of southern Korea dispatched a delegation to the emperor of Japan to inform him of the truth of this new religion. A power struggle ensued at the court between those who favored the new beliefs and those who opposed them.

Finally, the opposition fell, and Buddhism became the official religion of Japan. The emperors used it to help them spread their power.

Both in China and in Japan, Buddhism established friendly relations with other religions. This was possible in the Orient where people assume that truth can be found in diverse ways, while it would have been inconceivable in the West where it is assumed that truth has only one face. In the West one could not be a Catholic and Protestant at the same time, or a Protestant and Muslim, or a Muslim and a Jew. In China one can be an adherent of Buddhism, Confucianism, and Taoism. In Japan one can be, and most people still are, Shintoists and Buddhists. But the basic tenets of these religions were similar in some aspect. The Lord Buddha could have uttered the following words: "There is no guilt greater than to sanction ignoble ambitions. There is no greater calamity than to be discontented with one's lot. There is no greater fault than the wish to be grasping. Contentment is enduring and unchanging." Or: "To those who are good to me, I am good, and to those who are not good to me, I am also good."

It was not Buddha who had said those things, but a sage in the Honan province of China under the Chu dynasty. His name was Lao-Tzu, and he proclaimed that right conduct and the eternal spirit of righteousness were the "road"—Tao. He became the founder of the religion known as Taoism, with which the teachings of Lord Buddha were linked.

Buddha could have also said that the cardinal virtues

were filial piety, benevolence, justice, propriety, intelligence, and fidelity. Yet, this was the teaching of K'ung Fu-tzu the philosopher, whom the world knows as Confucius. He founded a religion which, like Buddhism, has no gods with the features of men, but it has ethical principles and the virtues of morality. Buddhism and Confucianism have existed very well together in China, along with Taoism.

It was the same in Japan where Buddhism met Shintoism—"the way of the gods." While the traditionalist Brahmans in India recognized only four hundred million gods, in Japan the number of divinities was estimated at eight hundred billion, so that the entire universe was teeming with them—historical personages, spirits of the ancestors, and countless nature gods. Yet, Buddhism—with no man-made gods—and Shintoism—with its hundreds of billions of gods—are living side by side in the land.

In Asoka's reign, too, Buddhism and Brahmanism coexisted in India. The king himself saw no inconsistency in calling himself the "beloved of gods." Yet his heart was in Buddhism, which he saw as the incarnation of an ethical principle, the supremacy of truth.

To "live Buddhism," as Asoka interpreted it, was not easy. In the course of time Hinduism-Brahmanism, the old religion, regained its lost ground on the Indian peninsula.

The people of India evidently found it easier to pacify the forty crores of gods than to satisfy their own consciences. It was hard to discover the ultimate truth; easier to flatter the gods. Life in India seems to have been always exceptionally hard. People felt more comfortable if they could turn to a favorite god for aid in life's countless crises. Asoka meant well when he put his people under the surveillance of his morality officers, but who would want to be constantly watched over, even in the best cause? People in India felt more at home in the company of their familiar traditions. A thousand years after Asoka's death Buddhism went out of the life of the people of India. But it stayed and spread in the countries overland and overseas.

In the course of centuries, Muslim rulers swept into India, and beginning with the sixteenth century they established their supremacy over most of the subcontinent. Their religion was the opposite of that of the majority of their subjects. One god—Allah—was the ruler of their universe. Islam had more similarity with Buddhism than with Hinduism. Therefore, the Muslim rulers may have looked upon it as competition. Islam became a strong minority religion, while the majority of the people continued to serve their Hindu gods. By the middle of the twentieth century, Buddhism in India had become a miniscule sect. There were more Christians on the subcontinent than Buddhists.

But at the beginning of the twentieth century, Buddhism experienced a limited revival in India. Increasingly, it was embraced by casteless Hindus, who followed the example of the leader of these depressed people—Dr. B. R. Ambedkar, who had become a Buddhist.

Long after Asoka, Buddhism did penetrate into parts

of the West, too, particularly the Western hemisphere where it now has hundreds of thousands of followers. Particularly large is the following of Zen-Buddhism, which has been characterized by "concentration of thought on a given problem. . . . the intuitive grasp of truth, momentary ecstasy, and the sense of oneness with the ultimate real."

Contrary to the thinking of the Enlightened One, Buddha is worshiped as a god by his followers in many lands. In certain Buddhist countries a large number of superhuman figures fill the shrines—some of them with features to scare a child. Buddhism, as the guide to a moral life, does not always play the part assigned to it by its founder.

Even though India is no longer a Buddhist country, it looks with pride upon the times when the spirit of the Enlightened One ruled in the land. That is why King Asoka's charka, the wheel, is the emblem of the Republic of India today. It is a Buddhist symbol, representing the changing nature of fate and the eternity of life.

13

✻ DEATH AND A NEW LIFE

IN one of his famed inscriptions, King Asoka had boasted: "There is prosperity in all the world. There is peace and happiness on earth."

After the disastrous Kalinga War, he had built a vast empire upon the foundations of a world religion. An entire generation had grown up knowing no other king, and he had occupied his throne for nearly forty years. Now he was getting old and tired.

Life began to weigh heavily upon the king, and his preoccupation with religion interfered with his conduct of governmental affairs. Under his reign many monasteries had been built, and the one closest to his heart was

Kukkutarama. Many legends have survived in connection with it. We assume that these legends contain a seed of history, even though greatly distorted and woven into the fabrics of fancy.

In a moment of supreme elation, according to one legend, the king vowed to donate a thousand million gold pieces to Buddha's service. Part of the money was transferred to the monastery and part of it employed for missionary work. It seems that Asoka had large amounts of funds transferred from the royal treasury. In a few months the government vaults were nearly depleted, and the officials began to worry. How were they, and the numerous morality officers of the king, to be paid? It was no use to talk to the king himself, who now lived in a world of dreams. So the officers of the state approached his grandson, Samprati, presumed to be Asoka's heir.

"O, prince," the ministers wailed, "soon the treasury will be unable to meet even the most urgent needs of thy illustrious sire. It is thy duty, O prince, to put an end to the drain of gold."

The prince, being a loyal grandson, made an attempt to penetrate the mind of the king, but the old man could not be reached. He merely wanted to help the missionaries and his favorite monks. So, the prince undertook to order the treasurer not to transfer additional funds at the king's behest.

Unable to obtain gold from the royal vault, Asoka now began to give away the valuable plates that graced the royal tables. Recalling the government's obligation to the people and the needs of the social services, the courtiers tried to talk to him again, but it was no use. The gold plates gone, the king started to give away the embossed silver services. Eventually, all the palace treasures were gone, and the royal tables were furnished with iron vessels, until the king gave those to the monks also. They were replaced with the cheapest clay.

King Asoka began to realize what was going on when he was no longer able to carry on his charitable work. He summoned his ministers into his inner chambers and asked them, with tears in his eyes:

"Tell me, who is the ruler of this land?"

"Your Majesty is the ruler," the ministers replied.

While bitter tears continued to flow from his eyes, Asoka once more addressed the courtiers.

"Why do you say this, since you know this is not true? Do you say it out of the goodness of your hearts? How low have I fallen from my lofty estate. Save this half-apple I have naught." And he showed the half-apple to the palace crowd.

Then he issued instructions that the half-apple be taken to the Kukkutarama monastery, using the following words:

"Behold, the king of India has come to this pass. Stripped of health, vigor and earthly goods he has no support save the Assembly of the Saints [the monastery]. This fruit he offers to you so that the entire Assembly may partake of it. This will be his last gift."

After a while, the king called his chief minister, Radhagupta, and again he asked: "Who is the sovereign of this land?"

"Sire," the chief minister replied, "Your Majesty is the sovereign of this land."

The king replied, as his mind began to clear for the moment: "This earth enwrapped by the ocean in its glorious sapphire garment, this land whereof the face is adorned with many jewels and gems; this soil sustaining all creatures and Mount Madura . . . all of this I bequeath to the Assembly of Saints. As a reward for this good deed I ask not for the privilege of dwelling in the palace of either Indra or Brahma, nor do I crave the felicity of kingship, which is fleeting, anyway, and is gone swifter than the running water. The reward I crave for the abiding faith prompting me to convey this gift is self-control, esteemed by saints and exempted from change."

As was his custom, Asoka sealed the deed of the gift with the imprints of his teeth. Thus he bequeathed the universe—which he claimed to possess—to the Assembly of Saints.

To "redeem the earth" from the greedy "saints," the ministers had to find forty million gold pieces, according to the ancient tale.

Having sealed the deed, the king had performed the last official act of his reign. Then Asoka "fulfilled the law of mortality." He died about 232 B.C.; the date is not certain.

Because Asoka had lost interest in the business of the government, his domain had fallen apart toward the end of his reign. It is thought that he deeded parts of his realm to his next of kin. One of his sons received Kashmir and was reputed to have been an active and vigorous king, like his father. He expelled intruders and conquered the plains as far as Kanauj. This son reverted to the faith of the ancestors, however, worshiping Siva and the Divine Mothers, in whose honor he and his spouse, Isadanevi, erected many shrines. He was actually hostile to Buddhism.

Who followed Asoka on the throne of Pataliputra? The record is not clear. It may have been the grandson, Samprati. Or it may have been another grandson, Dasaratha. Whoever it was, a time of trouble followed Asoka's death. Six years was the average reign of his successors. The last ruler of the Maurya dynasty was Brihadratha, who was assassinated by his commander in chief, Pushyamitra, in 185 B.C. For one hundred and ten years thereafter the throne was occupied by members of the assassin's Sunga dynasty.

During the new time of troubles that arose, Greek-led troops penetrated into the land from Bactria, in the northwest, as did Parthians, headed by Demetrius I, Apollodotus of Artemita, and Menander. "Apollodotus conquered more [Indian] tribes than Alexander [the Great]," wrote Strabo the Greek historian, "as he crossed the Hypanis to the east and advanced to the Isamus. . . ."

Of these rulers, Menander was called not only the

Great King, but also *Soter*—the just. He ruled for a long time, and the Buddhists extolled him because he had embraced their creed. Greeks occupied Pataliputra.

Other foreign dynasties followed, as India seemed to fall apart. But the peninsula showed amazing powers of resilience and kept bouncing back. It was a time of wars, dissensions, disintegration, and attempts at unification. The Gupta monarchy followed in the fourth century of the Christian era. Again India seemed on its way back.

Asoka's physical realm had fallen apart, and much of his work was discarded. Yet, Asoka's influence never waned, and the radiance of his name was never dimmed. Throughout India's history, for more than two thousand years, three names have stood out above all others, and all three had fallen under the spell of the Magadha king. One was Akbar the Great, who flourished in the sixteenth century. The other two were immortals of the twentieth century—Mahatma Gandhi, the spiritual founder of the modern Indian republic, and Jawaharlal Nehru, its first prime minister.

The career of Akbar shows remarkable similarities with that of Asoka. Akbar was neither Hindu nor Buddhist, but a Muslim. However, like his famous predecessor, he was broad-minded in religious affairs. He had many schools erected for Hindus and other sects, too. He had a number of representative Hindu religious books translated from the original Sanskrit into Persian, the language of the court. Also, he married a Hindu princess and wore the Zoroastrians' "sacred girdle." In those days, the dreadful *suttee* was still in vogue. This was the custom to have widows cremate themselves on their dead husbands' funeral pyres. Akbar banned this inhuman practice. He also forbade the marriages of children. He invited Christian missionaries to the land, and gathered a group of brilliant men at his court. All faiths, in his eyes, were of equal worth. In turn, he was admired by people of other creeds as, for instance, a visiting Jesuit priest, who extolled his virtues and called him a most unusual monarch.

Gandhi's inspiration was also Asoka. Like the ancient king, Gandhi believed that mankind could be saved only if it turned to the tenets of ahimsa, nonviolence. Wars, Gandhi held, never solved problems, except perhaps for short periods. Violence was bound to beget more violence. Gandhi held that only *satyagraha*—soulforce, the steadfast grasping of truth—could solve problems. He learned from Asoka that truth was god and god was truth. He also learned that truth was the force that regulated the processes of life. As long as religions upheld truth, they all were equally true.

Nehru, the first prime minister of the Republic of India, was also Asoka's disciple. Unlike the king of Magadha, Nehru followed no set creed. Yet, he was a deeply religious man, who dedicated his life to the service of his countrymen and, especially, of the poor.

Indian history is thus interwoven with Asoka's influence. No other man throughout the ages has so left his mark upon the people of the subcontinent. That is why the India of today has selected the symbols of his belief as its own emblems. Generations after his death, Asoka is still alive in India. King Asoka remains an inspiration to his people, who form the most populous democracy in the world today. Truly, Asoka the Great is an immortal of history.

CHRONOLOGY

All dates B.C. and approximate

INDEX